Strategic Intervention Teacher Activity Guide

RtI Response to Intervention Tier 2 Activities

Grade 2

INCLUDES:
- Diagnostic Practice for Prerequisite Skills
- Activities for Students Needing Tier 2 Instructional Intervention
- Copying Masters

Printed in the U.S.A.

ISBN   978-0-544-24904-2

11   1026   22 21 20 19 18 17

4500651036   A B C D E F G

Contents

PROBLEM SOLVING STRATEGIES

© Houghton Mifflin Harcourt Publishing Company

Tier 2 and Tier 3 Intervention Resources

Using the Tier 2 and Tier 3 print and online Intervention resources help children build a solid foundation of mathematical ideas and concepts. *Go Math! Response to Intervention ·Tier 2 Activities* are designed for children who need small group instruction to review prerequisite concepts and skills needed for the chapter. *Go Math! Response to Intervention · Tier 3 Activities* are targeted at children who need one-on-one instruction to build foundational skills for the chapter. By focusing on essential prerequisite skills and concepts for each chapter, the tiered intervention skills prescribe instruction to prepare children to work successfully on grade-level content. The *Go Math! Response to Intervention · Tier 2 Activities, Response to Intervention · Tier 3 Activities*, and *Personal Math Trainer* resources help you accommodate the diverse skill levels of your children at all levels of intervention.

How do I determine if a child needs intervention?

Before beginning each chapter, have children complete the *Show What You Know* page in the *Go Math!* Student Edition. *Show What You Know* targets the prerequisite skills necessary for success in each chapter and allows you to diagnose a child's need for intervention. Alternatively, at the beginning of the school year, the Prerequisite Skills Test in the *Assessment Guide* can be used.

In what format are the intervention materials?

A. *Go Math! Response to Intervention · Tier 2 Activities* include the *Strategic Intervention Teacher Activity Guide*, which includes copying masters for skill development and skill practice and teacher support pages. The copying masters can be used by individual children or small groups. The teacher support pages provide teaching suggestions for skill development, as well as an Alternative Teaching Strategy for children who continue to have difficulty with a skill.

B. *Go Math! Response to Intervention · Tier 3 Activities* include the *Intensive Intervention Teacher Guide* and *Intensive Intervention Skill Packs* for Grades K–6. A separate *User Guide/Activity Guide* correlates *Intensive Intervention* Tier 3 skills and an Alternative Teaching Activity to each chapter of the *Go Math!* program.

C. *Personal Math Trainer* provides online skill development, and practice for all levels of intervention in an electronic format. *Personal Math Trainer* features pre-built assignments for intervention and practice. Children receive feedback on incorrect answers and learning aids help them develop clear insight into underlying concepts as they build toward an understanding of on-level skills.

Using Response to Intervention • Tier 2 Activities

What materials and resources do I need for intervention?

The teaching strategies may require the use of common classroom manipulatives or easily gathered classroom objects. Since these activities are designed only for those children who show weaknesses in their skill development, the quantity of materials will be small. For many activities, you may substitute materials, such as paper squares for tiles, coins for two-color counters, and so on.

How are the skill lessons in *Response to Intervention • Tier 2 Activities* structured?

Each skill lesson in the Teacher Activity Guide includes two student pages, a page of teacher support, and an answer key for the student pages.

The student lesson begins with *Learn the Math* — a guided page that provides a model or an explanation of the skill.

The second part of the lesson is *Do the Math* — a selection of exercises that provide practice and may be completed independently, with a partner, or with teacher direction. This page provides scaffolded exercises, which gradually remove prompts.

Children who have difficulty with the *Do the Math* exercises may benefit from the Alternative Teaching Strategy activity provided on the teacher support page of each lesson.

How can I organize my classroom and schedule time for intervention?

You may want to set up a Math Skill Center with a record folder for each child. Based on a child's performance on the *Show What You Know* page, assign prescribed skills by marking the child's record folder. The child can then work through the intervention materials, record the date of completion, and place the completed work in a folder for your review. Children might visit the Math Skill Center for a specified time during the day, two or three times a week, or during free time. You may wish to assign children a partner, assign a small group to work together, or work with individuals one-on-one.

Grade 2
Strategic Intervention: Response to Intervention • Tier 2
Chapter Correlations

Skill Number	Skill Title	*SWYK Chapter
1	Tens	Number Concepts
3	Place Value: 2-Digit Numbers	Numbers to 1,000
4	Compare 2-Digit Numbers Using Symbols	Numbers to 1,000
5	Sums to 10	Basic Facts and Relationships
6	Doubles and Doubles Plus One	Basic Facts and Relationships
7	Addition Facts	2-Digit Addition; Data
8	Tens and Ones	2-Digit Addition; 2-Digit Subtraction
9	Subtraction Facts	2-Digit Subtraction; Data
10	Read a Tally Chart	Data
12	2-Digit Addition	3-Digit Addition and Subtraction
13	Hundreds, Tens, and Ones	3-Digit Addition and Subtraction
16	Use Nonstandard Units to Measure Length	Length in Customary Units; Length in Metric Units
17	Measure Length Twice: Nonstandard Units	Length in Customary Units; Length in Metric Units
21	Time to the Hour	Money and Time
22	Identify Shapes	Geometry and Fraction Concepts
24	Use a Hundred Chart to Count	Number Concepts
25	Skip Count by Fives and Tens	Money and Time
26	Identify Three-Dimensional Shapes	Geometry and Fraction Concepts

*SWYK refers to the *Show What You Know* page at the beginning of each chapter.

Objective
To model and count groups of 10

Vocabulary

ones The value of a digit in the ones position on a place value chart

tens The value of a digit in the tens position on a place value chart; 1 ten = 10 ones

Manipulatives
connecting cubes

COMMON ERROR

- Children may think of a digit's place value when telling how many tens there are. So, instead of saying there are 2 tens, they may say there are 20 tens.

- To correct this, emphasize that children should look at the number of groups of ten and use that number to tell how many tens there are.

Learn the Math page IN3 Guide children through the examples. In Example 1, ask: **How many ones are in the group on the left?** 10 ones Say: **You can describe the group as 10 ones or as 1 ten.** Ask: **How many ones are in the group in Example 2?** 20 ones **How many groups of 10 can you make?** 2 groups of ten Say: **You can describe the group as 20 ones or as 2 tens.**

Read the directions for Exercise 1. Demonstrate on the board for children how to draw a quick picture for a group of ten ones. In Exercise 1 have them draw 3 tens and write the numbers.

REASONING Explain to children that 1 ten equals 10 ones. Ask: **How many tens are equal to forty ones?** 4 tens

Do the Math page IN4 Model Exercise 1 with children. If children are having difficulty identifying the correct number of tens that is equal to the given number of ones, have them draw each group of 10 as they count.

Assign Exercises 2–3 and monitor children's work.

For Problem 4, explain to children that when objects are placed in groups of ten, they are easier to count. Encourage children to draw tens or use connecting cubes in groups of ten to stand for the marbles. Then have children write the number of tens.

Children who make more than 1 error in Exercises 1–4 may benefit from the **Alternative Teaching Strategy**.

Alternative Teaching Strategy

Materials: paper clips or other classroom objects

Have partners sort simple classroom objects into groups of ten. For example, give different amounts of paper clips or other classroom objects to each pair. Encourage partners to work together to connect the paper clips into groups of ten. Then have children count how many tens they have as well as the total number of paper clips. Invite partners to exchange their objects with another pair to repeat the activity.

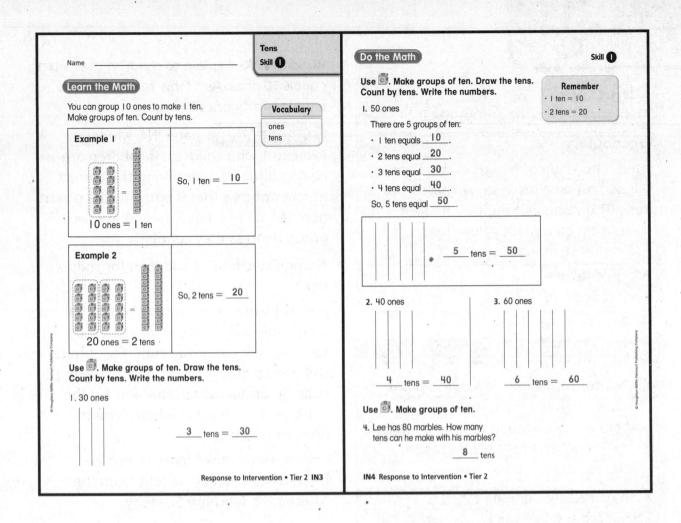

Learn the Math

Name _____

You can group 10 ones to make 1 ten.
Make groups of ten. Count by tens.

Vocabulary

ones
tens

Example 1

So, 1 ten = __10__

10 ones = 1 ten

Example 2

So, 2 tens = __20__

20 ones = 2 tens

Use ⬚. Make groups of ten. Draw the tens.
Count by tens. Write the numbers.

1. 30 ones

__3__ tens = __30__

Response to Intervention • Tier 2 **IN3**

Do the Math

Skill ①

Use ⬚. Make groups of ten. Draw the tens.
Count by tens. Write the numbers.

1. 50 ones

There are 5 groups of ten:

- 1 ten equals __10__.
- 2 tens equal __20__.
- 3 tens equal __30__.
- 4 tens equal __40__.
So, 5 tens equal __50__.

__5__ tens = __50__

Remember
- 1 ten = 10
- 2 tens = 20

2. 40 ones

__4__ tens = __40__

3. 60 ones

__6__ tens = __60__

Use ⬚. Make groups of ten.

4. Lee has 80 marbles. How many
tens can he make with his marbles?

__8__ tens

Name _____

Learn the Math

You can group 10 ones to make 1 ten.
Make groups of ten. Count by tens.

Example 1

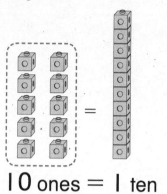

10 ones = 1 ten

So, 1 ten = _____.

Example 2

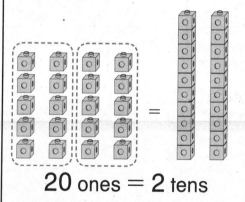

20 ones = 2 tens

So, 2 tens = _____.

Use 🔲**. Make groups of ten. Draw the tens.
Count by tens. Write the numbers.**

1. 30 ones

_____ tens = _____

Use ⬜. Make groups of ten. Draw the tens. Count by tens. Write the numbers.

1. 50 ones

There are 5 groups of ten:

- 1 ten equals _____.

- 2 tens equal _____.

- 3 tens equal _____.

- 4 tens equal _____.

So, 5 tens equal _____.

_____ tens = _____

2. 40 ones

_____ tens = _____

3. 60 ones

_____ tens = _____

Use ⬜. Make groups of ten.

4. Lee has 80 marbles. How many tens can he make with his marbles?

_____ tens

Compare 2-Digit Numbers
Skill 2

Objective
To compare 2-digit numbers

Vocabulary
is greater than More in quantity or amount
is less than Fewer in quantity or amount
is equal to Has the same value

Manipulatives
base-ten blocks

COMMON ERROR

- Children may confuse less than and greater than.
- To correct this, point out that less than means fewer and greater than means more.

Learn the Math page IN7 Discuss the concepts of "is greater than", "is less than", and "is equal to" with children. Guide children through Step 1. Point out that 10 ones is equal to 1 ten. Ask: **Why do the models make comparing numbers easier?** The models let us see how many tens and ones are in each number to compare. **Why compare the tens first?** If a ten is greater than another ten, then you do not need to compare the ones.

In Step 2, ask: **Why compare the ones?** Compare the ones because the tens are equal.

In Step 3, ask: **What can you say about the number whose ones are greater?** It is the greater number.

REASONING Ask: **Why don't you have to compare the ones if one number has more tens?** Tens have a greater place value than ones. The number with more tens is the greater number.

Do the Math page IN8 Model Exercise 1 with children and demonstrate how to solve the first bullet.

At the second bullet, ask: **Do you need to compare the ones? Explain.** Yes, I need to compare the ones because the tens are the same.

Assign Exercises 2–5 and monitor children's work.

Encourage children to use base-ten blocks to model Problem 6. Help children to compare 29 to each number choice and then choose the number that matches the clues.

Children who make more than 1 error in Exercises 1–6 may benefit from the **Alternative Teaching Strategy**.

Alternative Teaching Strategy
Manipulatives and Materials: base-ten blocks, index cards

Partners will write 2-digit comparison sentences and then model them with base-ten blocks. Give each child an index card on which to write a comparison sentence such as, "24 is greater than 15." Then have children give their card to their partner to model the comparison with base-ten blocks. When partners have made successful models, encourage pairs to exchange their index cards with another pair and repeat the activity.

Name _____

Learn the Math

You can use place value to compare numbers.

Write **is greater than**, **is less than**, or **is equal to**.

Vocabulary
is greater than
is less than
is equal to

23 ____?____ 26.

Step 1 Compare the tens. Are the tens the same? _yes_ 2 tens **is equal to** 2 tens.	23 26
Step 2 Compare the ones. Are the ones the same? _no_ 3 ones **is less than** 6 ones.	23 26
Step 3 Write **is greater than**, is less than, or is equal to.	23 is less than 26.

Do the Math

Write **is greater than, is less than, or is equal to.**

Remember
· Compare the tens.
· If the tens are the same, compare the ones.

1.

40 ____?____ 41.

· Compare the tens.
  Are the tens the same? _yes_
· Compare the ones.
  Are the ones the same? _no_
  0 ones _is less than_ 1 one.

So, 40 _is less than_ 41.

2. 25 _is greater than_ 13.

3. 54 _is greater than_ 45.

4. 32 _is less than_ 36.

5. 27 _is equal to_ 27.

Circle the answer that matches the clues.

6. Pat uses tens and ones to make the number 29.
   Mary makes a number that is less than 29.
   Which of these numbers could Mary make?

   39
   92
   ⑲

Name _____

Learn the Math

You can use place value to compare numbers.

Write **is greater than, is less than,** or **is equal to.**

Vocabulary

is greater than
is less than
is equal to

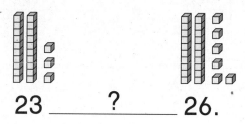

23 _____?_____ 26.

Step 1 Compare the tens. Are the tens the same? _____ 2 tens **is equal to** 2 tens.	23 26
Step 2 Compare the ones. Are the ones the same? _____ 3 ones **is less than** 6 ones.	23 26
Step 3 Write **is greater than, is less than,** or **is equal to.** 23 _____ 26.	23 26.

Write **is greater than, is less than,** or **is equal to.**

1.

40 _____?_____ 41

- Compare the tens.

   Are the tens the same? _____ .

- Compare the ones.

   Are the ones the same? _____

   0 ones _____ 1 one.

So, 40 _____ 41 .

2.

25 _____ 13.

3.

54 _____ 45.

4.

32 _____ 36.

5.

27 _____ 27.

Circle the answer that matches the clues.

6. Pat uses tens and ones to make the number 29.
   Mary makes a number that is less than 29.
   Which of these numbers could Mary make?

    39
    92
    19

Place Value: 2-Digit Numbers
Skill 3

Objective
To identify the place value of digits in 2-digit numbers .

Vocabulary
digits The symbols used in a numeration system; the ten digits are 0, 1, 2, 3, 4, 5, 6, 7, 8, and 9

Manipulatives
base-ten blocks

COMMON ERROR

- Children may not identify the correct number of tens and ones in a number.

- To correct this, use base-ten blocks to represent the number and point out, for example, that 25 can be described as 2 tens 5 ones.

Learn the Math page IN11 Read the introduction at the top of the page. Reinforce vocabulary that 0, 1, 2, 3, 4, 5, 6, 7, 8, and 9 are digits. Ask: **What are some 2-digit numbers you can make with these digits?** Answers may vary. Examples: 52, 75, 89 Explain that we know the value of a digit by its place. Review the example. Ask: **How many tens are in 23?** 2 tens. **How do you know the value of the digit 2 is 20?** The digit 2 is in the tens place and there are 2 tens, or 20. **How many ones are in 23?** 3 ones Ask: **How do you know the value of the digit 3 is 3?** The digit 3 is in the ones place and there are 3 ones, or 3.

Assign Exercises 1–2. Ask: **What is the value of the digit 7 in the number 76?** 70

REASONING Say: **Suppose Eva says that the value of the 4 in 43 is 4.** Ask: **Do you agree?** Possible answer: I do not agree. The digit 4 is in the tens place. It has a value of 40. Point out that Eva confused the value of the tens place and the value of the ones place.

Do the Math page IN12 Read and discuss Exercise 1 with children. Ask: **What place values do the base-ten blocks show?** tens and ones Guide them to determine the value of each set of blocks. Ask: **What number do the base-ten blocks show?** 54

Assign Exercises 2–5 and monitor children's work.

Have children read the riddle in Problem 6. Have them use the numbers at the right to decide which number matches the clues.

Children who make more than 1 error in Exercises 1–6 may benefit from the **Alternative Teaching Strategy**.

Alternative Teaching Strategy
Manipulatives and Materials: base-ten blocks, paper bags, paper

Children will pull base-ten blocks from paper bags to form 2-digit numbers. Give each pair a paper bag labeled "tens" containing tens and a paper bag labeled "ones" containing ones. Invite one partner to pull a few blocks from the ones bag and write the value. For example, a child may pull 3 ones and write, "3 ones." Have the other partner pull a few base-ten blocks from the tens bag and write the value, "4 tens." Then have partners use place value to write the number, for example, "43." Have children return the base-ten blocks to the bags and repeat the activity.

Learn the Math

0, 1, 2, 3, 4, 5, 6, 7, 8, and 9 are ___digits___.

In a 2-digit number, you know the value of a digit by its place.

Vocabulary

digits

Tens	Ones

Tens	Ones
2	3

2 tens **3** ones
23

The digit 2 is in the tens place. This means the value is 2 tens, or 20.

Tens	Ones

Tens	Ones
2	3

2 tens **3** ones
2**3**

The digit 3 is in the ones place. This means the value is 3 ones, or 3.

Circle the value of the underlined digit.

I. 7<u>6</u>

⑥   60

2. <u>4</u>3

㊵   4

Do the Math

I. I have 5 tens and 4 ones. What number am I?

- How many tens are there? ___5___ tens
- What is the value of the digit 5? ___50___
- How many ones are there? ___4___ ones
- What is the value of the digit 4? ___4___

So, I am the number ___54___

Remember
- You know the value of a digit by its place.
- A 0 in the ones place means there are 0 ones. 40 is 4 tens 0 ones.

Circle the value of the underlined digit.

2. <u>3</u>7

㉚   3

3. <u>4</u>8

⑧   80

4. 6<u>5</u>

50   ⑤

5. <u>7</u>2

7   ㊵

Circle the number that matches the clues.

6. My number has more tens than ones. One of the digits is 4. One of the digits is 8.

48 or ㊴

Name _____

Learn the Math

0, 1, 2, 3, 4, 5, 6, 7, 8, and 9 are _____.

In a 2-digit number, you know the value of a digit by its place.

Vocabulary

digits

Tens	Ones
2	3

2 tens **3** ones

23

The digit 2 is in the tens place. This means the value is 2 tens, or 20.

Tens	Ones
2	3

2 tens **3** ones

2**3**

The digit 3 is in the ones place. This means the value is 3 ones, or 3.

Circle the value of the underlined digit.

1. 7<u>6</u>

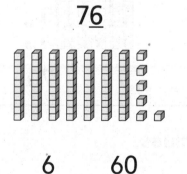

6   60

2. <u>4</u>3

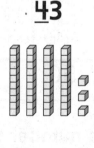

40   4

1. I have 5 tens and 4 ones.
   What number am I?

> **Remember**
> - You know the value of a digit by its place.
> - A 0 in the ones place means there are 0 ones. 40 is 4 tens 0 ones.

- How many tens are there? _____ tens

- What is the value of the digit 5? _____

- How many ones are there? _____ ones

- What is the value of the digit 4? _____

So, I am the number _____.

Circle the value of the underlined digit.

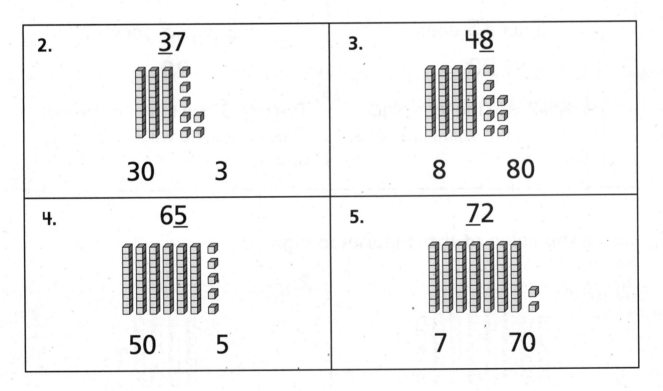

2.   3<u>7</u>

30   3

3.   4<u>8</u>

8   80

4.   6<u>5</u>

50   5

5.   <u>7</u>2

7   70

Circle the number that matches the clues.

6. My number has more tens than ones.
   One of the digits is 4.
   One of the digits is 8.

48   or   84

Compare 2-Digit Numbers Using Symbols
Skill 4

Objective
To compare 2-digit numbers using >, <, or =

Vocabulary
is greater than > A symbol used to compare two numbers, with the greater number given first

is less than < A symbol used to compare two numbers, with the lesser number given first

is equal to = A symbol used to show that two amounts have the same value

Manipulatives
base-ten blocks

COMMON ERROR

- Children may confuse the greater than and less than symbols when comparing numbers.

- To correct this, explain to children that the symbol always opens towards the greater number and the symbol always points to the smaller number.

Learn the Math page IN15 Read and discuss the problem with children. Guide them through Step 1. Point out that 10 unit cubes equal 1 base-ten rod. Ask: **Why do the base-ten blocks make comparing numbers easier?** because models let us see how many tens and ones are in each number

In Step 2, ask: **Why compare the tens first?** because the number with more tens is the greater number

In Step 3, ask: **When do you have to compare the ones?** when the tens are equal

REASONING Say: Anthony has 23 trading cards and Tara has 32 trading cards. Anthony says he has more cards. Ask: **Do you agree?** Possible answer: I do not agree. First, I start by comparing the tens. 3 tens is greater than 2 tens, so Tara has more cards.

Do the Math page IN16 Read and discuss Exercise 1 with children. Ask: **What are you trying to find out?** which person has more money **How does money relate to place value?** Cents can be shown in tens and ones.

Assign Exercises 2–4 and monitor children's work.

Children who make more than 1 error in Exercises 1–4 may benefit from the **Alternative Teaching Strategy**.

Alternative Teaching Strategy
Using overhead play money, lay out two sets of coins, each with dimes and pennies. Tell the children that you will be using dimes and pennies. The dimes represent the tens place of a 2-digit number. The pennies represent the ones place of a 2-digit number.

Have two children come up and count out the total amount for each group of coins. Ask: **How many dimes, or tens, are in each set? How can you compare the amounts? Do we need to compare the pennies?**

Explain to children how to use >, <, or = to record the comparison of two numbers.

Compare 2-Digit Numbers Using Symbols

Skill **4**

Learn the Math

Jacob has 42 crayons and Emma has 47 crayons. Who has more crayons?

Use ▭ ▫ to compare the tens and ones.

Vocabulary

is greater than >
is less than <
is equal to =

Step 1 Use ▭ ▫ to show each number.	42 47
Step 2 Compare the tens.	=
Step 3 Compare the ones.	2 _is less than_ 7. 2 ⊂ 7 Which number is greater? _47_

So, _Emma_ has more crayons.

Do the Math

Skill **4**

1. Joel has 54¢ in his coin bank. Latasha has 51¢ in her coin bank. Who has more money?

54 ◯ 51

Remember
· Compare the tens.
· If the tens are equal, compare the ones.

· Compare the tens. 5 ⊜ 5
· Compare the ones. 4 ⊝ 1
· Compare the numbers.   54 _is greater than_ 51.
54 ⊝ 51

So, _Joel_ has more money.

Write is greater than, is less than, or is equal to. Then write >, <, or =.

2.   43 _is equal to_ 43.
43 ⊜ 43

3.   28 _is less than_ 37.
28 ⊝ 37

Use ▭ ▫ and draw to show each number.

4. Agatha's brother weighs 26 pounds. Selena's brother weighs 23 pounds. Whose brother weighs less?

Selena's

Children should draw a group of 2 tens 6 ones and a group of 2 tens 3 ones.

Name _____

Learn the Math

Jacob has 42 crayons and Emma has
47 crayons. Who has more crayons?

Use ▱▱▱▱ ▱ **to compare the
tens and ones.**

Vocabulary

is greater than >
is less than <
is equal to =

Step 1 Use ▱▱▱▱ ▱ to show each number.	42 47
Step 2 Compare the tens.	=
Step 3 Compare the ones.	2 <u>is less than</u> 7. 2 ◯ 7 Which number is greater? _____

So, _____ has more crayons.

1. Joel has 54¢ in his coin bank. Latasha has 51¢ in her coin bank. Who has more money?

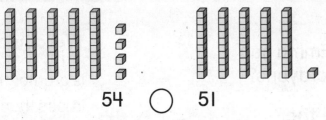

54 ◯ 51

- Compare the tens. 5 ◯ 5
- Compare the ones. 4 ◯ 1
- Compare the numbers.   54 _____ 51.

54 ◯ 51

So, _____ has more money.

Write is greater than, is less than, or is equal to. Then write >, <, or =.

2.

43 _____ 43.

43 ◯ 43

3.

28 _____ 37.

28 ◯ 37

Use ▭ ▱ and draw to show each number.

4. Agatha's brother weighs 26 pounds. Selena's brother weighs 23 pounds. Whose brother weighs less?

_____

Objective
To find sums to 10 in horizontal and vertical addition sentences

Vocabulary
sum The answer to an addition problem

Manipulatives
connecting cubes

COMMON ERROR

- Children may not know where to write the sum without an equal sign in a vertical addition sentence.

- To correct this, explain to children that the sum is written below the line.

Learn the Math page IN19 Have children look at the first model. Say: **You can add across.** Ask: **How many white cubes are there?** 2 white cubes **How many gray cubes are there?** 5 gray cubes **How many cubes are there in all?** 7 cubes Have children look at the second model. Say: **You can add down.** Ask: **How many white cubes are there?** 2 white cubes **How many gray cubes are there?** 5 gray cubes **How many cubes are there in all?** 7 cubes Ask: **How are these two problems different?** Possible answer: one problem adds across and the other problem adds down. **How are they alike?** Possible answer: they both use the same numbers to add, and have the same answer.

Assign Exercises 1–4. Guide children to see that they can add across or down and the sum stays the same.

REASONING Ask: **Why are the sums the same for both models in a row?** Possible answer: the sums are the same because both models use the same numbers.

Do the Math page IN20 Have children look at the horizontal model in Exercise 1. Ask: **How many cubes are there in all?** 7 cubes Then have children look at the vertical model and ask: **How many cubes are there in all?** 7 cubes For the vertical problem, guide children to write the sum below the line.

Assign Exercises 2–13 and monitor children's work.

Guide children to read Problem 14 to find that the total number of toy cars is 6. Encourage children to use connecting cubes to solve the problem.

Children who make more than 4 errors in Exercises 1–14 may benefit from the **Alternative Teaching Strategy**.

Alternative Teaching Strategy
Manipulatives and Materials: two-color counters, paper

Children will use two-color counters to represent addends in vertical addition sentences. Write one vertical addition sentence on the left side of a sheet of paper. Have children place red counters next to the first addend and yellow counters next to the second addend. Then have children count to find the total number of counters and write the sum. Guide children to write the sum below the line in the problem.

Sums to 10
Skill **5**

Learn the Math

You can add down or across.
The sum is the same.

Vocabulary

sum

Add across.	Write the sum.
	$2 + 5 = \underline{7}$
Add down.	Write the sum.
	$\begin{array}{r} 2 \\ + 5 \\ \hline 7 \end{array}$

Use ▦. Write the sum.

1.	2.
$3 + 2 = \underline{5}$	$\begin{array}{r} 3 \\ + 2 \\ \hline 5 \end{array}$
3.	4.
$2 + 4 = \underline{6}$	$\begin{array}{r} 2 \\ + 4 \\ \hline 6 \end{array}$

Do the Math

Skill **5**

Use ▦. Write the sum.

1.

Count the white cubes. $\underline{4}$ cubes

Count the gray cubes. $\underline{3}$ cubes

You can add across.

$4 + 3 = \underline{7}$

How many in all? $\underline{7}$ cubes

Remember

You can add across or down. The sum is the same.

You can add down.

$\begin{array}{r} 4 \\ + 3 \\ \hline 7 \end{array}$

How many in all?
$\underline{7}$ cubes

2. $\begin{array}{r} 3 \\ + 6 \\ \hline 9 \end{array}$	3. $\begin{array}{r} 4 \\ + 4 \\ \hline 8 \end{array}$	4. $\begin{array}{r} 1 \\ + 5 \\ \hline 6 \end{array}$	5. $\begin{array}{r} 5 \\ + 3 \\ \hline 8 \end{array}$
6. $\begin{array}{r} 6 \\ + 0 \\ \hline 6 \end{array}$	7. $\begin{array}{r} 4 \\ + 5 \\ \hline 9 \end{array}$	8. $\begin{array}{r} 2 \\ + 6 \\ \hline 8 \end{array}$	9. $\begin{array}{r} 6 \\ + 4 \\ \hline 10 \end{array}$
10. $\begin{array}{r} 8 \\ + 1 \\ \hline 9 \end{array}$	11. $\begin{array}{r} 3 \\ + 7 \\ \hline 10 \end{array}$	12. $\begin{array}{r} 7 \\ + 2 \\ \hline 9 \end{array}$	13. $\begin{array}{r} 0 \\ + 4 \\ \hline 4 \end{array}$

* 14. There are 3 toy cars in a box and 3 toy cars on a shelf. How many toy cars are there in all?

$\underline{6}$ toy cars

Name _____

Learn the Math

You can add down or across.
The sum is the same.

Vocabulary

sum

Add across.	Write the sum.
	$2 + 5 = \underline{\hphantom{00}}$
Add down.	Write the sum.
	$\begin{array}{r} 2 \\ +\ 5 \\ \hline \end{array}$

Use ⬚. Write the sum.

1.

$3 + 2 = \underline{\hphantom{00}}$

2.

$\begin{array}{r} 3 \\ +\ 2 \\ \hline \end{array}$

3.

$2 + 4 = \underline{\hphantom{00}}$

4.

$\begin{array}{r} 2 \\ +\ 4 \\ \hline \end{array}$

Use 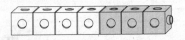 **. Write the sum.**

1.

Count the white cubes. _____ cubes

Count the gray cubes. _____ cubes

You can add across.

$$4 + 3 = \underline{\hspace{1cm}}$$

How many in all? _____ cubes

You can add down.

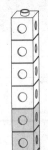

$$\begin{array}{r} 4 \\ + 3 \\ \hline \end{array}$$

How many in all?

_____ cubes

2. $\begin{array}{r} 3 \\ + 6 \\ \hline \end{array}$	3. $\begin{array}{r} 4 \\ + 4 \\ \hline \end{array}$	4. $\begin{array}{r} 1 \\ + 5 \\ \hline \end{array}$	5. $\begin{array}{r} 5 \\ + 3 \\ \hline \end{array}$
6. $\begin{array}{r} 6 \\ + 0 \\ \hline \end{array}$	7. $\begin{array}{r} 4 \\ + 5 \\ \hline \end{array}$	8. $\begin{array}{r} 2 \\ + 6 \\ \hline \end{array}$	9. $\begin{array}{r} 6 \\ + 4 \\ \hline \end{array}$
10. $\begin{array}{r} 8 \\ + 1 \\ \hline \end{array}$	11. $\begin{array}{r} 3 \\ + 7 \\ \hline \end{array}$	12. $\begin{array}{r} 7 \\ + 2 \\ \hline \end{array}$	13. $\begin{array}{r} 0 \\ + 4 \\ \hline \end{array}$

14. There are 3 toy cars in a box and 3 toy cars on a shelf. How many toy cars are there in all?

_____ toy cars

Doubles and Doubles Plus One

Skill 6

Objective

To use doubles and doubles plus one as strategies to find sums

Vocabulary

doubles An addition fact in which both addends are the same number, such as 2 + 2 and 5 + 5

doubles plus one A near doubles fact in which one addend is one greater than the other, such as 2 + 3 and 5 + 6

Manipulatives

connecting cubes

COMMON ERROR

- Children may double the greater addend when applying the doubles-plus-one strategy.

- To correct this, emphasize that they need to double the lesser addend and then add 1.

Learn the Math page IN23 Explain to children that the doubles strategy is helpful when two of the same number are being added. Guide children through the first example. Have them count the connecting cubes in the model and complete the addition sentence. Ask: **Why is this strategy called "doubles"?** Possible answer: it is called "doubles" because two of the same number are added. Then explain that the doubles-plus-one strategy is helpful when one number is one greater than the other number. Discuss how the lesser addend is doubled and then one more is added to find the sum. Guide children through the second

example. Have them count the connecting cubes in the model and complete the addition sentence. Ask: **Why is this strategy called "doubles plus one"?** Possible answer: it is called "doubles plus one" because the lesser number is doubled and one more is added. Assign Exercises 1–2. Ask: **What is the doubles fact that you can use to help find 3 + 4?** Possible answer: 3 + 3 = 6

REASONING Discuss with children that by knowing the doubles facts, they can also find the sum of twice as many facts by using the doubles-plus-one strategy.

Do the Math page IN24 Assist children by modeling Exercise 1 with them. Ask: **How do you know that this is a doubles-plus-one fact?** One number is one more than the other.

Assign Exercises 2–5 and monitor children's work.

For Problem 6, encourage children to use connecting cubes to model the 3 books Diane has and the 4 books Mei has. Elicit that they have 7 books in all.

Children who make more than 1 error in Exercises 1–6 may benefit from the **Alternative Teaching Strategy**.

Alternative Teaching Strategy

Manipulatives: connecting cubes

Have partners use connecting cube trains to model the relationship between doubles and doubles-plus-one facts. Have one partner build a connecting cube train using fewer than 9 cubes. Then have the other partner build the same amount plus one more. Have partners write the addition sentences for the models, for example 8 + 9 = 17.

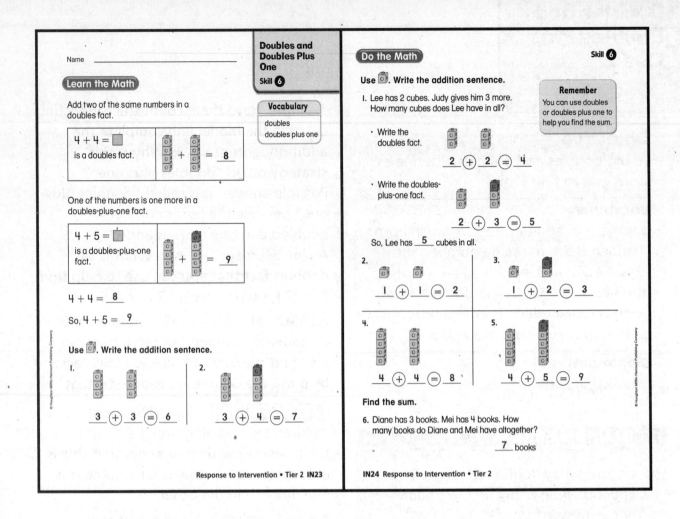

Name _____

Learn the Math

Add two of the same numbers in a doubles fact.

$4 + 4 = \square$
is a doubles fact.

$\square + \square = \underline{8}$

One of the numbers is one more in a doubles-plus-one fact.

$4 + 5 = \square$
is a doubles-plus-one fact.

$\square + \square = \underline{9}$

$4 + 4 = \underline{8}$

So, $4 + 5 = \underline{9}$.

Use □. Write the addition sentence.

1.

$3 (+) 3 (=) 6$

2.

$3 (+) 4 (=) 7$

Vocabulary

doubles
doubles plus one

Response to Intervention • Tier 2 **IN23**

Do the Math

Use □. Write the addition sentence.

1. Lee has 2 cubes. Judy gives him 3 more. How many cubes does Lee have in all?

- Write the doubles fact.

$2 (+) 2 (=) \underline{4}$

- Write the doubles-plus-one fact.

$2 (+) 3 (=) \underline{5}$

So, Lee has __5__ cubes in all.

2.

$1 (+) 1 (=) 2$

3.

$1 (+) 2 (=) 3$

4.

$4 (+) 4 (=) 8$

5.

$4 (+) 5 (=) 9$

Find the sum.

6. Diane has 3 books. Mei has 4 books. How many books do Diane and Mei have altogether?

__7__ books

Remember

You can use doubles or doubles plus one to help you find the sum.

IN24 Response to Intervention • Tier 2

Name _____

Learn the Math

Add two of the same numbers in a doubles fact.

Vocabulary

doubles

doubles plus one

$4 + 4 = $ ☐

is a doubles fact.

☐ + ☐ = ____

One of the numbers is one more in a doubles-plus-one fact.

$4 + 5 = $ ☐

is a doubles-plus-one fact.

☐ + ☐ = ____

$4 + 4 = $ ____

So, $4 + 5 = $ ____.

Use ⬛. Write the addition sentence.

1.

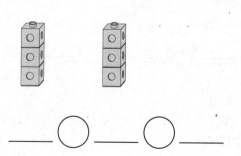

____ ◯ ____ ◯ ____

2.

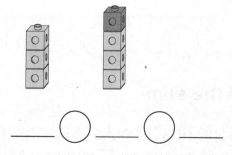

____ ◯ ____ ◯ ____

Do the Math

Use . Write the addition sentence.

1. Lee has 2 cubes. Judy gives him 3 more. How many cubes does Lee have in all?

 • Write the doubles fact.

 • Write the doubles-plus-one fact.

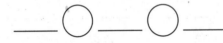

So, Lee has _____ cubes in all.

2.

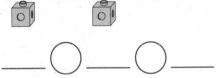

3.

4.

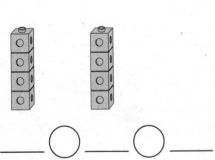

5.

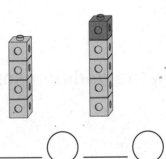

Find the sum.

6. Diane has 3 books. Mei has 4 books. How many books do Diane and Mei have altogether?

_____ books

Addition Facts

Skill 7

Objective
To practice addition facts

Vocabulary

sums The answers to addition problems

addends Any of the numbers that are added

COMMON ERROR

- Children may not know under what circumstances they can use each addition strategy.

- To correct this, review the criteria for each addition strategy as well as examples of how to use it.

Learn the Math page IN27 Read and discuss the examples with children. Review each addition strategy with children and have them explain when they could use each one. Ask: **When do you use the rule of adding zero?** when one of the addends is a zero **When do you use doubles plus one?** when one of the addends is one more than the other **When do you use doubles minus one?** when one of the addends is one less than the other **If you change the order of the addends to help you solve a problem, will it change the sum?** no

Have children complete Exercises 1–6. Encourage children to name the strategy they used for each pair of problems. Invite children to provide examples of when they would use each strategy.

REASONING Ask: **What is a way to find the sum of 8 + 7? Is there another way? Explain.** Possible answers: use doubles plus one: since $7 + 7 = 14$, then $7 + 8 = 15$; use doubles minus one: since $8 + 8 = 16$, then $8 + 7 = 15$

Do the Math page IN28 Read and discuss Exercise 1 with children. Ask: **What numbers are you adding together to find the sum?** 6 and 7 **What doubles fact can you use?** Possible answer: $6 + 6 = 12$ with the strategy doubles plus one, or $7 + 7 = 14$ with the strategy doubles minus one

Assign Exercises 2–13 and monitor children's work.

Guide children to read Problem 14 and find that the addends are 4 and 4. Elicit that the sum is 8. Invite volunteers to explain the strategy they used to solve the problem.

Children who make more than 4 errors in Exercises 1–14 may benefit from the **Alternative Teaching Strategy.**

Alternative Teaching Strategy

Manipulatives and Materials: counters, numeral cards 0–9 (see *Teacher Resources*)

Partners will work together to find sums using the strategies they have learned. Provide children with counters and a set of numeral cards 0–9. Display the list of strategies from student page IN27. Have one partner select two numeral cards to add together. The other partner chooses a strategy and together they find the sum. Invite children to use counters to model the problems. Encourage partners to try other possible strategies.

Learn the Math

These are some ways to remember sums.

Adding zero	Doubles	Order of addends
$4 + 0 = 4$	$7 + 7 = 14$	$6 + 4 = 10$
$5 + 0 = 5$	Doubles plus one	$4 + 6 = 10$
$6 + 0 = 6$	$7 + 8 = 15$	
$7 + 0 = 7$	Doubles minus one	$3 + 9 = 12$
$8 + 0 = 8$	$7 + 6 = 13$	$9 + 3 = 12$
Any number plus zero equals that number.	Changing one of the addends by 1 changes the sum by 1.	Changing the order of the addends does not change the sum.

Write the sum.

1. $8 + 8 = 16$	2. $2 + 7 = 9$	3. $0 + 6 = 6$
$8 + 9 = 17$	$7 + 2 = 9$	$4 + 0 = 4$
4. $8 + 4 = 12$	5. $3 + 0 = 3$	6. $9 + 9 = 18$
$4 + 8 = 12$	$0 + 5 = 5$	$9 + 8 = 17$

Do the Math

1. Danny has 6 orange slices. Ted has 7 orange slices. How many slices do they have in all?

- Danny has __6__ slices. Ted has __7__ slices.

- Write an addition sentence for the problem.

  __6__ + __7__ = __?__

- What doubles fact can you use? __6__ + __6__ = __12__

  __6__ + __7__ = __13__

So, Danny and Ted have __13__ slices in all.

Write the sum.

2. $7 + 0 = 7$	3. $4 + 4 = 8$	4. $7 + 5 = 12$
$3 + 0 = 3$	$4 + 3 = 7$	$5 + 7 = 12$
5. $6 + 6 = 12$	6. $8 + 2 = 10$	7. $9 + 0 = 9$
$6 + 7 = 13$	$2 + 8 = 10$	$0 + 5 = 5$
8. $0 + 8 = 8$	9. $7 + 8 = 15$	10. $5 + 5 = 10$
$3 + 0 = 3$	$8 + 7 = 15$	$5 + 6 = 11$
11. $7 + 7 = 14$	12. $2 + 2 = 4$	13. $3 + 3 = 6$
$7 + 6 = 13$	$2 + 3 = 5$	$3 + 2 = 5$

14. Liza picks 4 flowers. Nicole picks the same number of flowers. How many flowers do they pick in all?   __8__ flowers

Name _____

Learn the Math

These are some ways to remember sums.

Adding zero	Doubles	Order of addends
$4 + 0 = \underline{4}$	$7 + 7 = \underline{14}$	$6 + 4 = \underline{10}$
$5 + 0 = \underline{5}$	Doubles plus one	$4 + 6 = \underline{}$
$6 + 0 = \underline{6}$	$7 + 8 = \underline{}$	
$7 + 0 = \underline{7}$	Doubles minus one	$3 + 9 = \underline{12}$
$8 + 0 = \underline{}$	$7 + 6 = \underline{}$	$9 + 3 = \underline{}$
Any number plus zero equals that number.	Changing one of the addends by 1 changes the sum by 1.	Changing the order of the addends does not change the sum.

Write the sum.

1. $8 + 8 = \underline{}$ $8 + 9 = \underline{}$	2. $2 + 7 = \underline{}$ $7 + 2 = \underline{}$	3. $0 + 6 = \underline{}$ $4 + 0 = \underline{}$
4. $8 + 4 = \underline{}$ $4 + 8 = \underline{}$	5. $3 + 0 = \underline{}$ $0 + 5 = \underline{}$	6. $9 + 9 = \underline{}$ $9 + 8 = \underline{}$

Do the Math

I. Danny has 6 orange slices. Ted has 7 orange slices. How many slices do they have in all?

- Danny has _____ slices. Ted has _____ slices.

- Write an addition sentence for the problem.

  _____ + _____ = _____?

- What doubles fact can you use? _____ + _____ = _____

- _6_ + _7_ = _____

So, Danny and Ted have _____ slices in all.

Write the sum.

2. $7 + 0 =$ _____ $3 + 0 =$ _____	3. $4 + 4 =$ _____ $4 + 3 =$ _____	4. $7 + 5 =$ _____ $5 + 7 =$ _____
5. $6 + 6 =$ _____ $6 + 7 =$ _____	6. $8 + 2 =$ _____ $2 + 8 =$ _____	7. $9 + 0 =$ _____ $0 + 5 =$ _____
8. $0 + 8 =$ _____ $3 + 0 =$ _____	9. $7 + 8 =$ _____ $8 + 7 =$ _____	10. $5 + 5 =$ _____ $5 + 6 =$ _____
11. $7 + 7 =$ _____ $7 + 6 =$ _____	12. $2 + 2 =$ _____ $2 + 3 =$ _____	13. $3 + 3 =$ _____ $3 + 2 =$ _____

14. Liza picks 4 flowers. Nicole picks the same number of flowers. How many flowers do they pick in all?

_____ flowers

Objective
To use the place value of digits to write numbers as tens and ones

Manipulatives and Materials
base-ten blocks, place-value charts

COMMON ERROR

- Children might reverse the digits when writing teen numbers. With 14, some children may write 41 because they hear the four first.

- To correct this, have children write teen numbers in place-value charts and use base-ten blocks to model each number.

Learn the Math page IN31 Read and discuss the model with children. Ask: **In which place is the digit 3 in the number 35?** the tens place **How many tens are there?** 3 tens **What is the value of 3 tens?** 30 **In which place is the digit 5 in the number 35?** the ones place **How many ones are there?** 5 ones **What is the value of 5 ones?** 5 **What is the value of 3 tens 5 ones?** 35

Work through the exercises below the model together, asking similar questions. Remind children that when working with teen numbers, to make sure there is 1 ten in the tens place.

Assign Exercises 1–2. Ask: **How do you know how many tens and ones to write for a number?** The digit in the tens place tells how many tens. The digit in the ones place tells how many ones.

REASONING Write the numbers 24 and 34 on the board. Tell children to model 24 and 34 with base-ten blocks. Ask: **How are 24 and 34 different?** Possible answer: 34 has one more ten. It is 10 more than 24. **How are 24 and 34 alike?** Possible answer: 24 and 34 both have 4 ones.

Do the Math page IN32 Discuss Exercise 1 with children. Ask: **How many tens do you see?** 3 tens **How many ones do you see?** 6 ones Have children fill in the blanks for the number of tens and ones. 3 tens 6 ones Ask: **What is the value of 3 tens?** 30 **What is the value of 6 ones?** 6

Assign Exercises 2–5 and monitor children's work.

Encourage children to use base-ten blocks to model Problem 6. Guide them to see that 29 is 2 tens 9 ones.

Children who make more than 1 error in Exercises 1–6 may benefit from the **Alternative Teaching Strategy**.

Alternative Teaching Strategy
Manipulatives and Materials: base-ten blocks, number cube labeled 1–6, index cards

Have one partner toss a number cube and write that digit on an index card. Have the other partner toss a number cube and write that digit on the same index card to form a 2-digit number. Then have partners use base-ten blocks to model and record the number of tens and ones. Provide partners with other index cards to repeat the activity.

Learn the Math

You can show a number as tens and ones.

Tens	Ones
3	5

The digit **3** in **35** has a value of 3 tens, or 30.

The digit **5** in **35** has a value of 5 ones, or 5.

Write the number. _____ 35

Write the number of tens and ones. __3__ tens __5__ ones

So, __35__ = __3__ tens __5__ ones.

Write the number. Then write the number of tens and ones.

1.

Tens	Ones

__14__ = __1__ ten __4__ ones

2.

Tens	Ones

__26__ = __2__ tens __6__ ones

Do the Math

Skill **8**

Write the number. Then write the number of tens and ones.

Remember
- Find the value of each digit.
- Find the number of tens and ones.

1.

- Write the number. __36__
- How many tens are there? __3__ tens
- How many ones are there? __6__ ones

So, __36__ = __3__ tens __6__ ones.

2.

__48__ = __4__ tens __8__ ones

3.

__17__ = __1__ ten __7__ ones

4.

__39__ = __3__ tens __9__ ones

5.

__23__ = __2__ tens __3__ ones

Use ▭ ▱ to solve.

6. Chad has 29 trading cards. How many groups of 10 trading cards can he make? __2__ groups of 10

How many trading cards will not be in groups of 10? __9__ trading cards

Name _____

Learn the Math

You can show a number as tens and ones.

Tens	Ones
3	5

The digit **3** in **3**5 has a value of 3 tens, or 30.

The digit **5** in 3**5** has a value of 5 ones, or 5.

Write the number.   35

Write the number of tens and ones.   3 tens   5 ones

So, 35 = _____ tens _____ ones.

Write the number. Then write the number of tens and ones.

1.

Tens	Ones

_____ = _____ ten _____ ones

2.

Tens	Ones

_____ = _____ tens _____ ones

Write the number. Then write the number of tens and ones.

1.

· Write the number. _____

· How many tens are there? _____ tens

· How many ones are there? _____ ones

So, _36_ = _____ tens _____ ones.

2.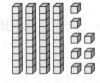

_____ = _____ tens _____ ones

3.

_____ = _____ ten _____ ones

4.

_____ = _____ tens _____ ones

5.

_____ = _____ tens _____ ones

Use ▭ ▢ **to solve.**

6. Chad has 29 trading cards. How many groups of 10 trading cards can he make?

_____ groups of 10

How many trading cards will not be in groups of 10?

_____ trading cards

Objective
To practice subtraction facts

Vocabulary

difference The answer to a subtraction problem

COMMON ERROR

- Children may not know under what circumstances they can use each subtraction strategy.

- To correct this, review the criteria for each subtraction strategy as well as how to use it.

Learn the Math page IN35 Read and discuss the examples with children. Review each subtraction strategy with them and have them explain when they could use each one. Ask: **When do you count back?** Count back when the number being subtracted is 1, 2, or 3. **When do you use addition to help you subtract?** I can use addition when I can think of a related addition fact. **When do you use another subtraction fact?** I use another subtraction fact when I know a subtraction fact in the same fact family. Guide children to complete the exercises at the bottom of the page. Have them name the strategy they would use for pairs of problems. Ask children to provide examples of types of problems they would use with each strategy.

REASONING Ask: Which strategy would you use to find the difference of $6 - 2$? **Is there another way?** Possible answer: I could count back 2: (6), 5, 4. I could also use another fact: $6 - 4 = 2$. Ask: **What is the difference?** 4

Do the Math page IN36 Read and discuss Exercise 1 with children. Ask: **What number are you subtracting to find the difference?** 3 **What strategy will you use to find the difference?** Possible answer: I can count back 3: (12), 11, 10, 9. The difference is 9.

Assign Exercises 2–13 and monitor children's work.

Read through Problem 14 with children. Encourage them to use a strategy to find the difference. Invite volunteers to explain the strategy they used to solve the problem.

Children who make more than 5 errors in Exercises 1–14 may benefit from the **Alternative Teaching Strategy.**

Alternative Teaching Strategy
Manipulatives: two-color counters

Children will use two-color counters to represent the numbers in a subtraction fact. Give children 20 two-color counters and write a subtraction sentence on the board, such as $14 - 6 =$ ___. Have children count out 14 red counters and then turn 6 over so that they are yellow. Children write the difference, 8, shown by the remaining red counters.

Learn the Math

These are some ways to find differences.

Vocabulary

difference

Count back.	Think addition.	Use another fact.
$9 - 3 = \blacksquare$	$10 - 6 = \blacksquare$	$11 - 5 = \blacksquare$
Say 9. Count back 3. 8, 7, 6	Think: $6 + \underline{4} = 10$	Think: $11 - \underline{6} = 5$
So, $9 - 3 = \underline{6}$ difference	So, $10 - 6 = \underline{4}$ difference	So, $11 - 5 = \underline{6}$ difference

Complete the number sentences.

1. $8 - 3 = \underline{5}$ $6 - 2 = \underline{4}$	2. $13 - 9 = \underline{4}$ $9 + \underline{4} = 13$	3. $12 - 4 = \underline{8}$ $12 - \underline{8} = 4$
4. $6 - 1 = \underline{5}$ $7 - 3 = \underline{4}$	5. $16 - 9 = \underline{7}$ $9 + \underline{7} = 16$	6. $15 - 8 = \underline{7}$ $15 - \underline{7} = 8$
7. $8 - 2 = \underline{6}$ $9 - 1 = \underline{8}$	8. $14 - 8 = \underline{6}$ $8 + \underline{6} = 14$	9. $17 - 9 = \underline{8}$ $17 - \underline{8} = 9$

Do the Math

Complete the number sentences.

1. Camila has 12 books. She gives 3 to Jon.
How many books does she have left?

 • Write the number of books Camila has. $\underline{12}$ books

 • Write the number of books given to Jon. $\underline{3}$ books

 • What is the difference? $\underline{9}$

 • $12 - 3 = \underline{9}$.

 So, Camila has $\underline{9}$ books left.

2. $10 - 2 = \underline{8}$ $8 - 1 = \underline{7}$	3. $13 - 6 = \underline{7}$ $13 - 7 = \underline{6}$	4. $15 - 9 = \underline{6}$ $9 + \underline{6} = 15$
5. $17 - 8 = \underline{9}$ $8 + \underline{9} = 17$	6. $7 - 2 = \underline{5}$ $10 - 2 = \underline{8}$	7. $9 - \underline{5} = 4$ $9 - 4 = \underline{5}$
8. $11 - 3 = \underline{8}$ $11 - 8 = \underline{3}$	9. $12 - 7 = \underline{5}$ $7 + \underline{5} = 12$	10. $9 - 3 = \underline{6}$ $8 - 2 = \underline{6}$
11. $9 - 2 = \underline{7}$ $10 - 1 = \underline{9}$	12. $13 - 8 = \underline{5}$ $8 + \underline{5} = 13$	13. $14 - 5 = \underline{9}$ $14 - \underline{9} = 5$

14. Mark's coat has 12 buttons. Then 4 buttons fall off.
How many buttons are left?

 $\underline{8}$ buttons

Name _____

Learn the Math

These are some ways to find differences.

Vocabulary

difference

Count back.	Think addition.	Use another fact.
$9 - 3 = \blacksquare$	$10 - 6 = \blacksquare$	$11 - 5 = \blacksquare$
Say 9. Count back 3. 8, 7, 6	Think: $6 + \underline{\quad} = 10$	Think: $11 - \underline{\quad} = 5$

So, $9 - 3 = \underline{\quad}$.
           difference
	So, $10 - 6 = \underline{\quad}$.
	           difference
		So, $11 - 5 = \underline{\quad}$.
		           difference

Complete the number sentences.

1. $8 - 3 = \underline{\quad}$ $6 - 2 = \underline{\quad}$	2. $13 - 9 = \underline{\quad}$ $9 + \underline{\quad} = 13$	3. $12 - 4 = \underline{\quad}$ $12 - \underline{\quad} = 4$
4. $6 - 1 = \underline{\quad}$ $7 - 3 = \underline{\quad}$	5. $16 - 9 = \underline{\quad}$ $9 + \underline{\quad} = 16$	6. $15 - 8 = \underline{\quad}$ $15 - \underline{\quad} = 8$
7. $8 - 2 = \underline{\quad}$ $9 - 1 = \underline{\quad}$	8. $14 - 8 = \underline{\quad}$ $8 + \underline{\quad} = 14$	9. $17 - 9 = \underline{\quad}$ $17 - \underline{\quad} = 9$

Complete the number sentences.

1. Camila has 12 books. She gives 3 to Jon.
   How many books does she have left?

   · Write the number of books Camila has. _____ books

   · Write the number of books given to Jon. _____ books

   · What is the difference? _____

   · $12 - 3 =$ _____.

   So, Camila has _____ books left.

2. $10 - 2 =$ _____
   $8 - 1 =$ _____

3. $13 - 6 =$ _____
   $13 - 7 =$ _____

4. $15 - 9 =$ _____
   $9 + $ _____ $= 15$

5. $17 - 8 =$ _____
   $8 + $ _____ $= 17$

6. $7 - 2 =$ _____
   $10 - 2 =$ _____

7. $9 - $ _____ $= 4$
   $9 - 4 =$ _____

8. $11 - 3 =$ _____
   $11 - 8 =$ _____

9. $12 - 7 =$ _____
   $7 + $ _____ $= 12$

10. $9 - 3 =$ _____
    $8 - 2 =$ _____

11. $9 - 2 =$ _____
    $10 - 1 =$ _____

12. $13 - 8 =$ _____
    $8 + $ _____ $= 13$

13. $14 - 5 =$ _____
    $14 - $ _____ $= 5$

14. Mark's coat has 12 buttons. Then 4 buttons fall off.
    How many buttons are left?

    _____ buttons

Objective
To read a tally chart and interpret the data

Vocabulary
tally chart A chart used to record information in an organized way using tally marks

tally mark A mark used to keep track of what has been counted

COMMON ERROR

- Some children may not draw the fifth tally mark across the previous four.

- To correct this, have children count aloud to five as they practice making groups of five marks. Explain that they should "draw mark five on its side."

Learn the Math page IN39 Read and discuss the problem with children. Guide them through Step 1. Draw one tally mark on the board and point out that one tally mark stands for 1. Draw five tally marks on the board (with the fifth tally mark "on its side") and point out that five tally marks stand for 5. Ask: **Why is the fifth tally mark on its side?** It shows that the 5 tally marks are a group. This makes them easier to count.

Emphasize that a tally chart is an easy way to show and compare different numbers of objects.

REASONING Ask: **How could you find which fruit more children chose without counting the tally marks?** Look to see which row has more. Point out that there is no group of five in the row for bananas, and there is one group of five in the row for apples. This is a quick way to see that more children chose apples.

Do the Math page IN40 Read and discuss Exercise 1 with children. Ask: **Do you have to count the tally marks to tell which month had the most games played?** No, by looking at the chart you can tell that more games were played in June. It is a good idea to count to be sure. Guide children to solve the problem.

Assign Exercises 2–5 and monitor children's work.

Children who make more than 1 error in Exercises 1–5 may benefit from the **Alternative Teaching Strategy.**

Alternative Teaching Strategy
Copy the chart below. Show children how counting by fives for each grouping and counting on by one for each single tally mark will result in the total. Write 5, 10, etc., below each grouping as you are counting the tally marks.

Favorite Pet	
Dog	ЖЖ ЖЖ ЖЖ
Cat	ЖЖ ЖЖ |||
Hamster	|||

Name _____

Learn the Math

Mrs. Timmel's class voted for their favorite fruit. Which fruit did more children vote for?

Favorite Fruit

apples	ЖⅡ III
bananas	III

Each tally mark I stands for one vote. ЖⅡ tally marks stand for 5 votes.

Step 1 How many children voted for **bananas**?	_3_ children voted for bananas.
Step 2 How many children voted for **apples**?	_8_ children voted for apples.
Step 3 Which fruit has **more votes**?	_8_ is greater than _3_. So more children voted for ___apples___ .

Do the Math

Skill **10**

Use the chart to answer each question.

1. Jack's softball team plays games in May, June and July. In which month does Jack have the most games?

Jack's Softball Games

May	ЖⅡ I
June	ЖⅡ ЖⅡ
July	ЖⅡ

• Count the tally marks. How many games are in May? _6_
• How many games are in June? _10_
• How many games are in July? _5_
So, Jack has the most games in __June__

2. In which month does Jack have the fewest games? __July__

3. How many games does Jack have in all? _21_

4. How many more games are there in June than in July? _5 more_

5. If five more tally marks were added to the month of May, which month would have the most games?
   __May__

Name _____

Learn the Math

Mrs. Timmel's class voted for their favorite fruit. Which fruit did more children vote for?

Favorite Fruit	
apples	卌 |||
bananas	|||

Each tally mark **|** stands for one vote. **卌** tally marks stand for 5 votes.

Step 1 How many children voted for **bananas**?	_____ children voted for bananas.
Step 2 How many children voted for **apples**?	_____ children voted for apples.
Step 3 Which fruit has **more votes**?	8 _____ is greater than _____. So more children voted for _____.

Use the chart to answer each question.

1. Jack's softball team plays games in May, June and July. In which month does Jack have the most games?

Jack's Softball Games	
May	ⵌⵌ I
June	ⵌⵌ ⵌⵌ
July	ⵌⵌ

> **Remember**
> - I tally mark stands for 1 vote.
> - ⵌⵌ tally marks stand for 5 votes.

- Count the tally marks. How many games are in May? _____

- How many games are in June? _____

- How many games are in July? _____

So, Jack has the most games in _____ .

2. In which month does Jack have the fewest games? _____

3. How many games does Jack have in all? _____

4. How many more games are there in June than in July? _____

5. If five more tally marks were added to the month of May, which month would have the most games?

_____

Skip Count by Twos
Skill 11

Objective
To skip count by twos

Vocabulary
skip count To count in a pattern that skips numbers

Manipulatives
connecting cubes

COMMON ERROR

- Children may not understand that they can skip count only when counting equal groups.

- To correct this, have children connect some cubes into equal groups of 2 and others into unequal groups. Have children find which groups are equal and which groups are not.

Learn the Math page IN43 Explain to children they can skip count when they see a pattern in numbers or objects. Explain that skip counting is a faster way to count. Instruct children to look at the pictures of the pairs of shoes. Ask: **How many shoes are in each pair?** 2 shoes Explain that because there are 2 shoes in each group, they can skip count by twos to find how many shoes Merriam has in all. Ask: **If you skip count by twos 6 times, what number do you stop on?** 12 Say: **So, Merriam has 12 shoes in all.**

Guide children to complete Example 2. Encourage children to skip count by twos 5 times to find the total number of pencils Jamal has. 10 pencils

Assign Exercises 1–2. Have children use connecting cubes.

REASONING Ask: **Why is skip counting easier than counting each number?** Possible answer: it is easier to count by skipping numbers because not every number is said, so it takes less time.

Do the Math page IN44 Guide children to solve Exercise 1. They may wish to use connecting cubes to model the problem. Instruct them to count the connecting cubes in one group to see that there are two in each group. Encourage children to skip count by twos to find the total number of connecting cubes, 12.

Assign Exercises 2–5 and monitor children's work.

For Problem 6, suggest that children draw 4 equal groups of two pennies or use connecting cubes to solve.

Children who make more than 1 error in Exercises 1–6 may benefit from the **Alternative Teaching Strategy**.

Alternative Teaching Strategy
Materials: number lines 0–10 (see *Teacher Resources*)

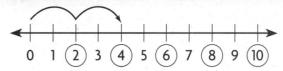

Children will use a number line to skip count by twos. Give children number lines 0–10. Ask: **If you skip count by twos, on what number do you start counting?** 0 Say: **Now skip count by twos.** Demonstrate this by counting 2 places from 0 and placing your pencil on 2. **What is the next number in the pattern?** 4 Continue skip counting by twos. Have children circle the numbers on their number lines as they count.

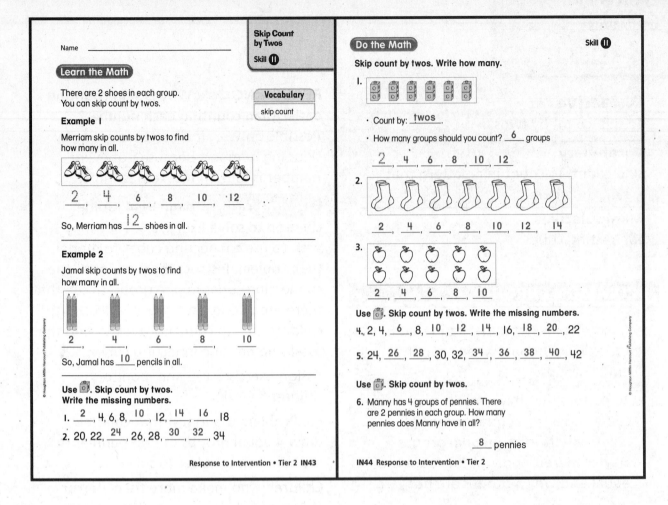

Name _____

Learn the Math

There are 2 shoes in each group.
You can skip count by twos.

Vocabulary

skip count

Example 1

Merriam skip counts by twos to find how many in all.

2, 4, 6, 8, 10, 12

So, Merriam has 12 shoes in all.

Example 2

Jamal skip counts by twos to find how many in all.

2, 4, 6, 8, 10

So, Jamal has 10 pencils in all.

**Use ⊡. Skip count by twos.
Write the missing numbers.**

1. 2, 4, 6, 8, 10, 12, 14, 16, 18
2. 20, 22, 24, 26, 28, 30, 32, 34

Do the Math

Skip count by twos. Write how many.

1.
   · Count by: twos.
   · How many groups should you count? 6 groups
   2, 4, 6, 8, 10, 12

2. 2, 4, 6, 8, 10, 12, 14

3. 2, 4, 6, 8, 10

Use ⊡. Skip count by twos. Write the missing numbers.

4. 2, 4, 6, 8, 10, 12, 14, 16, 18, 20, 22
5. 24, 26, 28, 30, 32, 34, 36, 38, 40, 42

Use ⊡. Skip count by twos.

6. Manny has 4 groups of pennies. There are 2 pennies in each group. How many pennies does Manny have in all?

   8 pennies

Name _____

Learn the Math

There are 2 shoes in each group.
You can skip count by twos.

Example 1

Merriam skip counts by twos to find
how many in all.

2 , 4 , ____ , ____ , ____ , ____

So, Merriam has __12__ shoes in all.

Example 2

Jamal skip counts by twos to find
how many in all.

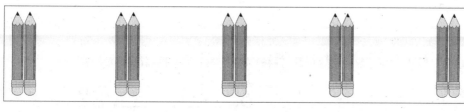

____ , ____ , ____ , ____ , ____

So, Jamal has ____ pencils in all.

Use 🎲. Skip count by twos.
Write the missing numbers.

1. ____, 4, 6, 8, ____, 12, ____, ____, 18

2. 20, 22, ____, 26, 28, ____, ____, 34

Skip count by twos. Write how many.

1.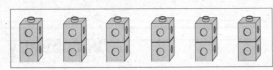

   · Count by: _____.

   · How many groups should you count? _____ groups

   2̶, _____, _____, _____, _____, _____

2.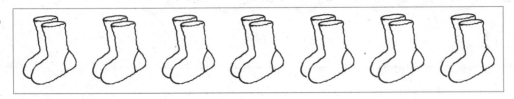

   _____, _____, _____, _____, _____, _____, _____

3.

   _____, _____, _____, _____, _____

Use ▦. Skip count by twos. Write the missing numbers.

4. 2, 4, _____, 8, _____, _____, _____, 16, _____, _____, 22

5. 24, _____, _____, 30, 32, _____, _____, _____, _____, 42

Use ▦. Skip count by twos.

6. Manny has 4 groups of pennies. There
   are 2 pennies in each group. How many
   pennies does Manny have in all?

   _____ pennies

Objective
To record sums for models of 2-digit addition with or without regrouping

Vocabulary
regroup An action that involves changing a number from one form into an equivalent form

Manipulatives
base-ten blocks

COMMON ERROR

- Children may add the tens first and end up with two digits in the ones place.

- To correct this, instruct children to cover the answer box in the tens place with their fingers. Once they have written the ones, they can uncover the tens box.

Learn the Math page IN47 Read the story problem with children. Guide them through Step 1. Help them to connect the numbers in the problem to the addends represented by the base-ten blocks.

In Step 2, ask: **Why do you need to regroup?** Possible answer: I need to regroup because there are enough ones to make a ten. Show children where to write 4 ones and the regrouped 1 ten.

For Step 3, guide them to add the tens and to also add the regrouped ten. Ask: **What is the sum of 16 + 28?** 44

REASONING Say: **Suppose Dan is adding 8 to 22. He says that there are not enough** ones to regroup. Ask: **Do you agree?** Possible answer: I do not agree. There are exactly 10 ones to regroup with 0 ones left over. Make sure children know that if they have more than 9 ones, they can regroup 10 ones as 1 ten.

Do the Math page IN48 Read the problem with children. Invite them to use base-ten blocks to model the problem. Guide them through the steps. Check to make sure that they know to write the regrouped ten in the tens column.

Ask: **What should you do if you cannot regroup?** I can add the ones and then add the tens.
Assign Exercises 2–7 and monitor children's work.

Read through Problem 8 with children. Ask: **Can you regroup?** yes Encourage children to model the problem with base-ten blocks. Invite them to draw a picture of the model to show their work.

Children who make more than 2 errors in Exercises 1–8 may benefit from the **Alternative Teaching Strategy**.

Alternative Teaching Strategy
Manipulatives and Materials: base-ten blocks, ten frame (see *Teacher Resources*)

Have children use a ten frame to help them model the addition. On the board, write a 2-digit addition problem that involves regrouping the ones. Have children model each addend with base-ten blocks. Then have them place the ones on a ten frame. When the ten frame is full, have them collect 1 ten while discarding 10 ones. Guide them to count the number of tens and ones and write the sum.

Name _____

Learn the Math

Darius drew 16 pictures. Greg drew 28 pictures.
How many pictures did they draw in all?

Vocabulary

regroup

Add. 16
    + 28

Step 1	Tens	Ones		Tens	Ones
Add the ones. Are there 10 ones to regroup? (yes) no				1	6
				+ 2	8
					☐

Step 2	Tens	Ones		Tens	Ones
Regroup. 14 ones is the same as 1 ten 4 ones. Write the regrouped ten. Write how many ones are in the ones place now.				1	
				1	6
				+ 2	8
					4

Step 3	Tens	Ones		Tens	Ones
Add the tens. Then write the tens.				1	
				1	6
				+ 2	8
				4	4

So, they drew __44__ pictures in all.

Do the Math

Regroup if you can. Write the sums.

Remember
Before you add, see if you can regroup.

1.
```
   22
 + 18
```

· Can you make a ten? __yes__

· Regroup 10 ones as __1__ ten.

· Write the regrouped ten.

· Write how many ones are in the ones place now.

· Add the tens. Then write the tens.

Tens	Ones
☐	
	2 2
+	1 8
4	0

2.
```
  1
  3  9
+ 3  8
  7  7
```

3.
```
  1
  1  8
+ 3  8
  5  6
```

4.
```
  1
  5  1
+ 1  3
  6  4
```

5.
```
  1
  24
+ 37
  61
```

6.
```
  42
+ 16
  58
```

7.
```
  1
  57
+ 28
  85
```

8. Jose has 24 marbles. Sandra gives him 18 marbles. How many marbles does Jose have in all?

__42__ marbles

Name _____

Learn the Math

Darius drew 16 pictures. Greg drew 28 pictures.
How many pictures did they draw in all?

Add.   1 6
          + 2 8

Step 1		
Add the ones. Are there 10 ones to regroup? (yes) no		Tens Ones 	Tens Ones ☐ 1 6 + 2 8

Step 2		
Regroup. 14 ones is the same as 1 ten 4 ones. Write the regrouped ten. Write how many ones are in the ones place now.		Tens Ones	Tens Ones 1 1 6 + 2 8 _____ 4

Step 3		
Add the tens. Then write the tens.		Tens Ones	Tens Ones 1 1 6 + 2 8 _____ 4 4

So, they drew _____ pictures in all.

Regroup if you can. Write the sums.

1.
$$\begin{array}{r} 22 \\ + \ 18 \\ \hline \end{array}$$

- Can you make a ten? _____

- Regroup 10 ones as _____ ten.

- Write the regrouped ten.

- Write how many ones are in the ones place now.

- Add the tens. Then write the tens.

Tens	Ones

Tens	Ones
☐	
2	2
+ 1	8

2.
$$\begin{array}{c|c} 3 & 9 \\ + 3 & 8 \\ \hline \end{array}$$

3.
$$\begin{array}{c|c} 1 & 8 \\ + 3 & 8 \\ \hline \end{array}$$

4.
$$\begin{array}{c|c} 5 & 1 \\ + 1 & 3 \\ \hline \end{array}$$

5.
$$\begin{array}{r} 24 \\ + \ 37 \\ \hline \end{array}$$

6.
$$\begin{array}{r} 42 \\ + \ 16 \\ \hline \end{array}$$

7.
$$\begin{array}{r} 57 \\ + \ 28 \\ \hline \end{array}$$

8. Jose has 24 marbles. Sandra gives him 18 marbles. How many marbles does Jose have in all?

_____ marbles

Hundreds, Tens, and Ones

Skill 13

Objective
To use place value of digits to write 3-digit numbers

Manipulatives
base-ten blocks

COMMON ERROR

- Children may forget the order of place value positions in 3-digit numbers.

- To correct this, remind children that the greatest place-value position is written first, and numbers are read from left to right.

Learn the Math page IN51 Read and discuss the model with children. Ask: **How many hundreds are there?** 2 hundreds Say: **So, 2 is written in the hundreds place. How many tens are there?** 3 tens Say: **So, 3 is written in the tens place. How many ones are there?** 8 ones Say: **So, 8 is written in the ones place. How do you write the number?** 238 Discuss with children the value of each digit in the number 238. Guide children as they complete Exercises 1–3.

REASONING Have children use base-ten blocks to model the number 462. Ask: **How are 462 and 562 different?** Possible answer: 562 has one more hundred than 462. Ask: **How are 462 and 562 alike?** Possible answer: both 462 and 562 have the same number of tens and ones.

Do the Math page IN52 Read and discuss Exercise 1 with children. Invite them to use base-ten blocks to model the number. Remind children to look at how many hundreds, tens, and ones are in the model and then write the number.

Assign Exercises 2–3 and monitor children's work.

In Problem 4, guide children to find the total number of beans James has in each of three bowls: 200, 90, and 5. Invite children to use base-ten blocks to model how many hundreds, tens, and ones are in each bowl and then write the number.

Children who make more than 1 error in Exercises 1–4 may benefit from the **Alternative Teaching Strategy.**

Alternative Teaching Strategy
Manipulatives and Materials: base-ten blocks, number cube, paper

Have children use base-ten blocks to model the number of hundreds, tens, and ones in 3-digit numbers. Have one partner toss a number cube three times while the other partner writes the digits to form a 3-digit number. Then have partners use base-ten blocks to model the number. Check that children's models match their number.

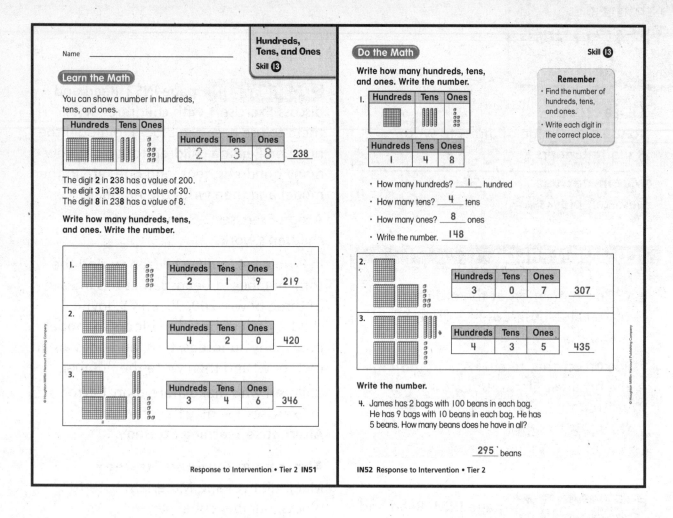

Name _____

Learn the Math

You can show a number in hundreds, tens, and ones.

Hundreds	Tens	Ones

Hundreds	Tens	Ones
2	3	8	238

The digit **2** in **2**38 has a value of 200.
The digit **3** in 2**3**8 has a value of 30.
The digit **8** in 23**8** has a value of 8.

Write how many hundreds, tens, and ones. Write the number.

1.

Hundreds	Tens	Ones
2	1	9	219

2.

Hundreds	Tens	Ones
4	2	0	420

3.

Hundreds	Tens	Ones
3	4	6	346

Do the Math

Skill **13**

Write how many hundreds, tens, and ones. Write the number.

1.

Hundreds	Tens	Ones

Hundreds	Tens	Ones
1	4	8

- How many hundreds? __1__ hundred
- How many tens? __4__ tens
- How many ones? __8__ ones
- Write the number. __148__

Remember
- Find the number of hundreds, tens, and ones.
- Write each digit in the correct place.

2.

Hundreds	Tens	Ones
3	0	7	307

3.

Hundreds	Tens	Ones
4	3	5	435

Write the number.

4. James has 2 bags with 100 beans in each bag. He has 9 bags with 10 beans in each bag. He has 5 beans. How many beans does he have in all?

__295__ beans

Name _____

Learn the Math

You can show a number in hundreds, tens, and ones.

Hundreds	Tens	Ones
(blocks)	(rods)	(dots)

Hundreds	Tens	Ones	
2	3	8	_____

The digit **2** in **2**38 has a value of 200.
The digit **3** in 2**3**8 has a value of 30.
The digit **8** in 23**8** has a value of 8.

Write how many hundreds, tens, and ones. Write the number.

1.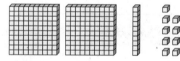

Hundreds	Tens	Ones	
			_____

2.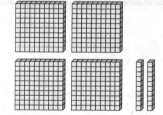

Hundreds	Tens	Ones	
			_____

3.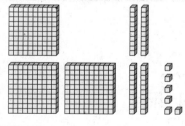

Hundreds	Tens	Ones	
			_____

Do the Math

Write how many hundreds, tens, and ones. Write the number.

Remember
· Find the number of hundreds, tens, and ones.
· Write each digit in the correct place.

I.

Hundreds	Tens	Ones

Hundreds	Tens	Ones

· How many hundreds? _____ hundred

· How many tens? _____ tens

· How many ones? _____ ones

· Write the number. _____

2.

Hundreds	Tens	Ones

_____

3.

Hundreds	Tens	Ones

_____

Write the number.

4. James has 2 bags with 100 beans in each bag. He has 9 bags with 10 beans in each bag. He has 5 beans. How many beans does he have in all?

_____ beans

Skip Count by Twos and Fives
Skill 14

Objective
To skip count using pictures

COMMON ERROR

- When skip counting, children may not realize that the number of items in the group and the number you are skip counting by will match up equally. It is important that children understand the purpose of skip counting.

- To correct this, explain to children that skip counting can be a shortcut for counting. Have children skip count by fives a group of 25 items. Show them that they can make groups of five. Then count 5, 10, 15, 20, 25.

Learn the Math page IN55 Read and discuss the problem with children. Guide them through Step 1. Point out that the skip-count unit is 5. Ask: **Why do models help when skip counting?** Possible answer: they help you to not lose track of your counting.

In Step 2, skip count the pennies aloud with children, pointing to each group as they count. Then skip count again as children trace or write the numbers below each group. Ask: **How do you know when to stop skip counting?** You stop skip counting at the last model, or last group, of items.

REASONING Say: **After skip counting a group of pennies by twos, Hailey says that her answer is 15 cents. Ask: Is this possible?** No; possible answer: if you are skip counting by twos, the answer has to be an even number. **Make sure children**

understand that the numbers between the skip-count numbers cannot be the answer.

Do the Math page IN56 Read Exercise 1 with children. Ask: **What are you trying to find out?** the number of baseballs in all Before writing any numbers, have children skip count the balls out loud, pointing to each group as they count.

Assign Exercises 2–4 and monitor children's work.

If children have difficulty writing the numbers, have them first skip count out loud.

Children who make more than 1 error in Exercises 1–4 may benefit from the **Alternative Teaching Strategy.**

Alternative Teaching Strategy
Arrange children in a line. Have them count off by ones and remember their numbers. As they count, have every fifth child step forward.

Explain that they have just counted by ones and they can count by fives, too. Point out that each of the children who stepped forward from the line is the fifth child in each group of five children. Count the five children in a couple of groups: 1, 2, 3, 4, **5**; 1, 2, 3, 4, **5**. Emphasize every fifth child as you count aloud.

Have the children who stepped forward say their numbers: 5, 10, 15, and so on.

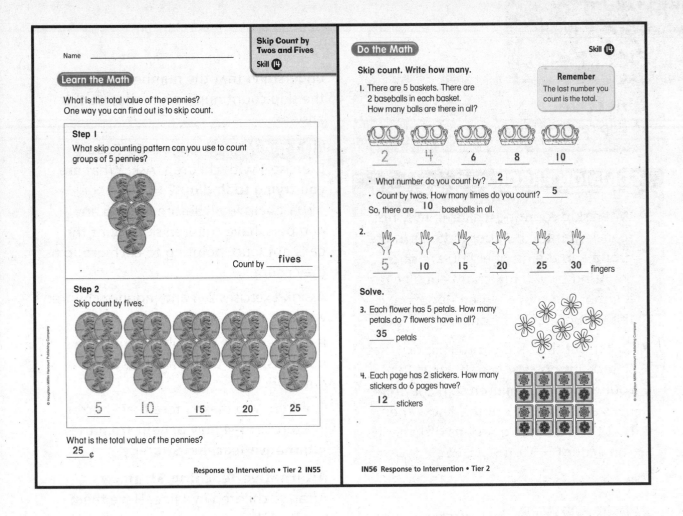

Learn the Math

Name _____

What is the total value of the pennies?
One way you can find out is to skip count.

Step 1

What skip counting pattern can you use to count groups of 5 pennies?

Count by _fives_

Step 2

Skip count by fives.

5   10   15   20   25

What is the total value of the pennies?
_25_ ¢

Do the Math

Skip count. Write how many.

Remember
The last number you count is the total.

1. There are 5 baskets. There are 2 baseballs in each basket. How many balls are there in all?

2   4   6   8   10

· What number do you count by? _2_
· Count by twos. How many times do you count? _5_
So, there are _10_ baseballs in all.

2.

5   10   15   20   25   30 fingers

Solve.

3. Each flower has 5 petals. How many petals do 7 flowers have in all?

_35_ petals

4. Each page has 2 stickers. How many stickers do 6 pages have?

_12_ stickers

Name _____

Learn the Math

What is the total value of the pennies?
One way you can find out is to skip count.

Step 1

What skip counting pattern can you use to count groups of 5 pennies?

Count by _____

Step 2

Skip count by fives.

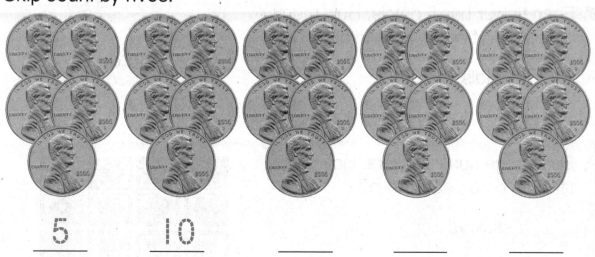

5   10   _____   _____   _____

What is the total value of the pennies?

_____¢

Skip count. Write how many.

1. There are 5 baskets. There are 2 baseballs in each basket. How many balls are there in all?

 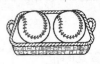

  2   4   _____   _____   _____

- What number do you count by? _____
- Count by twos. How many times do you count? _____

So, there are _____ baseballs in all.

2.

  5   _____   _____   _____   _____   _____ fingers

Solve.

3. Each flower has 5 petals. How many petals do 7 flowers have in all?

_____ petals

4. Each page has 2 stickers. How many stickers do 6 pages have?

_____ stickers

Draw to Show Addition
Skill 15

Objective
To draw a picture to solve a problem and write a matching addition sentence

COMMON ERROR

- Children may have difficulty seeing the two different addends in their drawings.

- To correct this, have children draw Xs for one addend and Os for the other addend, or use two different colors.

Learn the Math page IN59 Read the story problem at the top of the page with children. Ask: **What do you need to find out?** how many flowers are in the vase now Review the information in the story problem and have children circle the two quantities. Read Step 1 with children. Ask: **What does the shape represent?** Possible answer: the vase Continue guiding children through each step and have them trace as indicated. Ask: **What is drawn to represent the flowers?** Xs **How many Xs are there in all?** 7 **How do the Xs in the drawing relate to the numbers in the addition sentence?** The first Xs show the 3 flowers in the vase. The next 4 Xs show the flowers Lily put in.

Assign Exercise 1. Ask: **How many items in all are in your drawing?** 8

REASONING Ask: **How would your drawing be different if you were subtracting an amount?** Possible answer: I would show one amount and cross out the other amount rather than drawing more.

Do the Math page IN60 Read and discuss Exercise 1 with children. Ask: **What do you need to find to answer the question?** the total number of crackers on the plate now Guide children in completing Exercise 1. Ask: **How many crackers are in each group?** 7 and 2 **Which number answers the question?** the sum of the addition sentence; 9

Assign Exercises 2–3 and monitor children's work.

For Exercise 4, suggest that children make their drawings before answering the question.

Children who make more than 1 error in Exercises 1–4 may benefit from the **Alternative Teaching Strategy**.

Alternative Teaching Strategy
Manipulatives: two-color counters

Children will use two-color counters to represent the numbers in a story problem before drawing a picture. Write a story problem on the board, such as, *Jordan had 4 baseballs. His coach gave him 2 more baseballs. How many baseballs does Jordan have now?* Have children show the first addend with the red side of counters and show the second addend with the yellow side of more counters. Then have children make a simple drawing to represent each counter before writing the accompanying addition sentence.

Name _____

Learn the Math

There are 3 flowers in the vase.
Lily puts in 4 more flowers.
How many flowers are in the vase now?

You can draw a picture to help you solve a problem.

Step 1	
Draw a shape to show the vase.	(empty oval)
Step 2	
Draw Xs inside the shape to show the flowers.	XXX
Step 3	
Draw more Xs to show the added flowers.	XXX XXXX
Step 4	
Write a number sentence to match.	$\underline{3} + \underline{4} = \underline{7}$

Draw a picture. Write an addition sentence.

1. There are 5 oranges in a basket. Amy puts in 3 more oranges. How many oranges are in the basket in all?	Check children's drawings. $\underline{5} + \underline{3} = \underline{8}$

Draw a picture. Write an addition sentence.

Remember
· Draw one group.
· Then draw the other group.

1. There are 7 crackers on the plate.
   Ken puts 2 more crackers on the plate.
   How many crackers are on the plate now?

   · How many crackers are on the plate? _7_.

   · How many crackers are added? _2_.

   · Draw a picture.

   · The addition sentence is $\underline{7} + \underline{2} = \underline{9}$.

   So, there are _9_ crackers on the plate now.

2. Emma eats 8 grapes. Then she eats 2 more grapes. How many grapes does Emma eat altogether?	Check children's drawings. $\underline{8} + \underline{2} = \underline{10}$
3. There are 6 spoons on the table. Tim puts 1 more spoon on the table. How many spoons are on the table in all?	Check children's drawings. $\underline{6} + \underline{1} = \underline{7}$

Solve. Draw or write to show your work.

4. There are 4 glasses in the sink.
   Mr. West puts 4 more glasses into the sink.
   How many glasses in all are in the sink?

   _8_ glasses

Name _____

Learn the Math

There are 3 flowers in the vase.
Lily puts in 4 more flowers.
How many flowers are in the vase now?

You can draw a picture to help you solve a problem.

Step 1 Draw a shape to show the vase.	
Step 2 Draw Xs inside the shape to show the flowers.	
Step 3 Draw more Xs to show the added flowers.	
Step 4 Write a number sentence to match.	$\underline{\ 3\ } + \underline{\ 4\ } = \underline{\quad}$

Draw a picture. Write an addition sentence.

1. There are 5 oranges in a basket. Amy puts in 3 more oranges. How many oranges are in the basket in all?	$\underline{\quad} + \underline{\quad} = \underline{\quad}$

Draw a picture. Write an addition sentence.

1. There are 7 crackers on the plate.
Ken puts 2 more crackers on the plate.
How many crackers are on the plate now?

 · How many crackers are on the plate? _____.

 · How many crackers are added? _____.

 · Draw a picture.

 · The addition sentence is _____ + _____ = _____.

 So, there are _____ crackers on the plate now.

2. Emma eats 8 grapes. Then she eats 2 more grapes. How many grapes does Emma eat altogether?	_____ + _____ = _____
3. There are 6 spoons on the table. Tim puts 1 more spoon on the table. How many spoons are on the table in all?	_____ + _____ = _____

Solve. Draw or write to show your work.

4. There are 4 glasses in the sink.
Mr. West puts 4 more glasses into the sink.
How many glasses in all are in the sink?

 _____ glasses

Use Nonstandard Units to Measure Length

Skill 16

Objective
To measure length using nonstandard units

Manipulatives and Materials
color tiles, classroom objects

COMMON ERROR

- Children may not measure correctly when using nonstandard units.

- To correct this, explain to children that it is very important that they keep the units end-to-end rather than overlapped or spread apart. If the units are end-to-end, the measurement will be more accurate.

Learn the Math page IN63 Discuss with children the use of nonstandard units to measure length. Guide them through Step 1. Show children how to align the end of the tile with the end of the object. Point out that when using nonstandard units, it is very important to set the tiles end-to-end to measure the length.

In Step 2, ask: **Should there be a space in between your tiles?** no **Why not?** Tiles should be placed close together to get an accurate measurement.

In Step 3, have children count the number of tiles used to measure the length of the pencil. Ask: **About how long is the pencil?** The pencil is about 5 tiles long.

Invite children to measure the length of their own pencil using color tiles. Have them tell the length.

For Exercise 1, guide children to measure the length of a calculator, or another classroom object. Check that they set the tiles end to end along the length of the object.

REASONING Ask: **If your tiles are a little more than or a little less than the object you are measuring, what can you do?** I can use the number of units that is closer to the length of the object.

Do the Math page IN64 Read and discuss Exercise 1 with children. Ask: **How do you measure the stapler using tiles?** Possible answer: I set one tile at one end of the stapler and add more tiles until I reach the other end of the stapler.

Assign Exercises 2–4 and monitor children's work.

For Problem 5, encourage children to measure the length of each ribbon with color tiles. Have them circle the longer ribbon.

Children who make more than 1 error in Exercises 1–5 may benefit from the **Alternative Teaching Strategy**.

Alternative Teaching Strategy
Manipulatives and Materials: color tiles, masking tape, crayons

Place strips of masking tape on the table in front of partners and have them measure the length of the tape strips using color tiles. Have one partner place the first tile at one end of the tape. Have the other partner mark on the tape where the first tile ends. Encourage partners to take turns placing the next tile and drawing the line. When they have finished marking, have them count all the spaces to tell the length of the strip in color tiles.

© Houghton Mifflin Harcourt Publishing Company

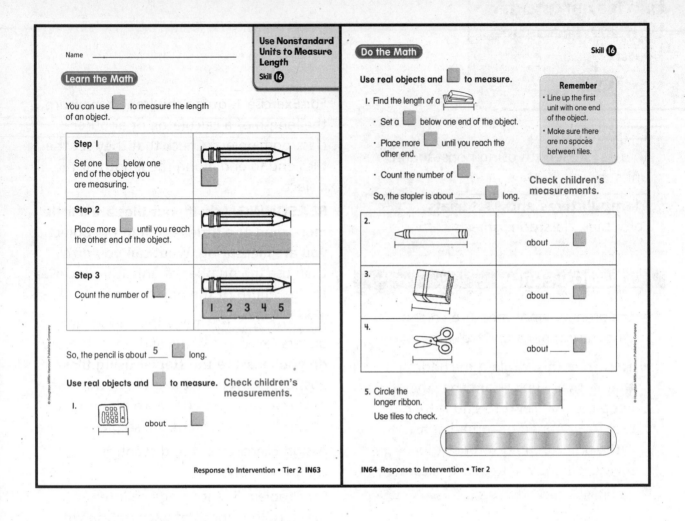

Name _____

Learn the Math

You can use ☐ to measure the length of an object.

Step 1	
Set one ☐ below one end of the object you are measuring. ☐	
Step 2	
Place more ☐ until you reach the other end of the object.	
Step 3	
Count the number of ☐.	1 2 3 4 5

So, the pencil is about ⁵ ☐ long.

Use real objects and ☐ **to measure.**   Check children's measurements.

I.

about _____ ☐

Do the Math

Skill 16

Use real objects and ☐ **to measure.**

I. Find the length of a

- Set a ☐ below one end of the object.
- Place more ☐ until you reach the other end.
- Count the number of ☐.

So, the stapler is about _____ ☐ long.

Remember
- Line up the first unit with one end of the object.
- Make sure there are no spaces between tiles.

Check children's measurements.

2.	about _____ ☐
3.	about _____ ☐
4.	about _____ ☐

5. Circle the longer ribbon.
   Use tiles to check.

Name _____

Learn the Math

You can use ⬜ to measure the length of an object.

Step 1 Set one ⬜ below one end of the object you are measuring.	
Step 2 Place more ⬜ until you reach the other end of the object.	
Step 3 Count the number of ⬜.	1 2 3 4 5

So, the pencil is about _____ ⬜ long.

Use real objects and ⬜ to measure.

1.

about _____ ⬜

Use real objects and ▢ **to measure.**

I. Find the length of a [stapler] .

  • Set a ▢ below one end of the object.

  • Place more ▢ until you reach the other end.

  • Count the number of ▢ .

So, the stapler is about _____ ▢ long.

> **Remember**
> • Line up the first unit with one end of the object.
> • Make sure there are no spaces between tiles.

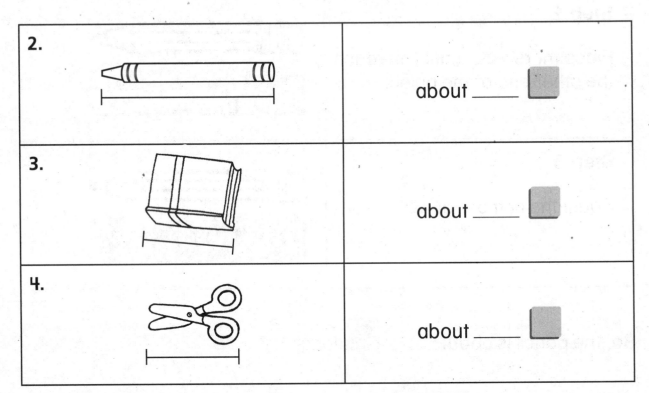

2. [crayon]	about _____ ▢
3. [eraser]	about _____ ▢
4. [scissors]	about _____ ▢

5. Circle the longer ribbon.

   Use tiles to check.

Objective
To measure length using two different nonstandard units

Manipulatives and Materials
connecting cubes, paper clips

COMMON ERROR

- Children may miscount the number of nonstandard units used.

- To correct this, have children set the nonstandard units end to end along the length of the object. Then have them point to each unit as they count aloud.

Learn the Math page IN67 Read and discuss the example with children. Guide them to use both types of nonstandard units to measure the same object twice. Ask: **About how many paper clips long is the flower?** The flower is about 2 paper clips long. **About how many connecting cubes long is the flower?** The flower is about 3 connecting cubes long. **Why are the two measurements different?** The two measurements are different because the paper clip and the connecting cube are different lengths. Ask, **If your measuring units are a little more than or a little less than the object, what can you do?** I can use the number of units that is closer to the length of the object. Guide children through Exercises 1–2. Remind them to use all paper clips or all connecting cubes when measuring the length of the ribbon.

REASONING Say: Suppose Jay and Shawn measure the length of a stapler. Jay says the stapler is 7 color tiles long. Shawn says the stapler is 9 connecting cubes long. Both Jay and Shawn are correct. How can this be true? The color tiles and the connecting cubes are different lengths.

Do the Math page IN68 Read and discuss Exercise 1 with children. Have them measure the eraser with paper clips. Then have them measure the eraser with connecting cubes. Tell children to line up cubes without using the tab of the cube.

Assign Exercises 2–5 and monitor children's work.

Read through Problem 6 with children. Have them measure the length of 1 cube (without the tab) at the end of the rope. Have them draw a line on the rope to show where to cut. Have them find and write the length of the rope after it is cut.

Children who make more than 1 error in Exercises 1–6 may benefit from the **Alternative Teaching Strategy**.

Alternative Teaching Strategy
Manipulatives and Materials: color tiles, connecting cubes, strips of paper

Have children trace nonstandard units, such as color tiles or connecting cubes, as they measure a strip of paper. Then have them count how many units they traced and write the number and unit. Have children repeat the activity using the same strip of paper but a different nonstandard unit.

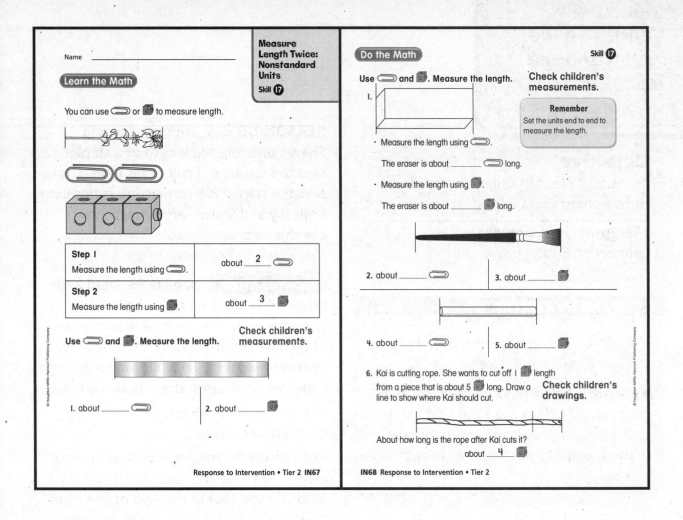

Learn the Math

Name _____

You can use ⬭ or ⬛ to measure length.

Step 1 Measure the length using ⬭.	about __2__ ⬭
Step 2 Measure the length using ⬛.	about __3__ ⬛

Use ⬭ and ⬛. Measure the length. **Check children's measurements.**

1. about _____ ⬭   2. about _____ ⬛

Do the Math

Skill 17

Use ⬭ and ⬛. Measure the length. Check children's measurements.

1.

- Measure the length using ⬭.

  The eraser is about _____ ⬭ long.

- Measure the length using ⬛.

  The eraser is about _____ ⬛ long.

Remember

Set the units end to end to measure the length.

2. about _____ ⬭   3. about _____ ⬛

4. about _____ ⬭   5. about _____ ⬛

6. Kai is cutting rope. She wants to cut off 1 ⬛ length from a piece that is about 5 ⬛ long. Draw a line to show where Kai should cut. **Check children's drawings.**

About how long is the rope after Kai cuts it?

about __4__ ⬛

Name _____

Learn the Math

You can use  or ◻ to measure length.

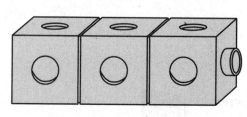

Step 1	
Measure the length using ⬭.	about _____ ⬭
Step 2	
Measure the length using ◻.	about _____ ◻

Use ⬭ and . Measure the length.

1. about _____ ⬭   2. about _____

Use 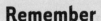 and ⬛. Measure the length.

1.

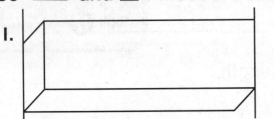

> **Remember**
> Set the units end to end to measure the length.

- Measure the length using ⬯.

  The eraser is about _____ ⬯ long.

- Measure the length using ⬛.

  The eraser is about _____ ⬛ long.

2. about _____ ⬯

3. about _____ ⬛

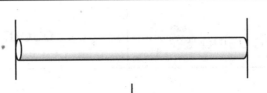

4. about _____ ⬯

5. about _____ ⬛

6. Kai is cutting rope. She wants to cut off 1 ⬛ length from a piece that is about 5 ⬛ long. Draw a line to show where Kai should cut.

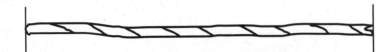

About how long is the rope after Kai cuts it?

about _____ ⬛

Use a Balance
Skill 18

Objective
To use nonstandard units and a balance to measure weight/mass

Vocabulary
balance An instrument used to compare weight/mass

Manipulatives and Materials
balance, connecting cubes, classroom objects

COMMON ERROR

- Children may become impatient with the balance and use their hands to stop the movement.

- To correct this, remind them to gently place a cube on the balance, and to wait for the balance to stop moving before adding another cube.

Learn the Math page IN71 Read and discuss the problem with children. Guide them through Step 1. Have them place a crayon on one pan of the balance. Point out that the balance is no longer level, or even. For Step 2, guide them to carefully place one connecting cube on the other pan. Ask: **Are the pans balanced?** no For Step 3, have children add cubes, one at a time, to the other pan until the pans balance. Ask: **If one more cube makes the pan go down lower than the pan on the other side, what can you do?** Possible answer: I can take off the cube and use the number of cubes on the pan as the closer measurement. Then ask: **So, about how many cubes does it take to balance a crayon?** Answers may vary.

Guide children through Exercises 1–2. Remind them to put the real object on one pan and then add connecting cubes, one at a time, to the other pan, stopping when the balance is level.

REASONING Say: **Suppose Sharon puts an orange on one side of a balance. Which side of the balance goes down?** The side with the orange goes down.

Do the Math page IN72 Read and discuss Exercise 1 with children. Guide them through the steps. Check that children are adding cubes one at a time. Ask: **How do you know when your object is balanced?** Possible answer: my object is balanced when both sides of the balance are level.

Assign Exercises 2–4 and monitor children's work.

For Problem 5, you may wish to provide children with real objects and a balance to help them choose the heaviest and lightest objects.

Children who make more than 1 error in Exercises 1–5 may benefit from the **Alternative Teaching Strategy.**

Alternative Teaching Strategy
Materials: classroom objects, paper

Have partners compare the difference among heavy and light objects. Give each pair two objects with which to compare. Have the first partner lift each object one at a time and later hold one object in each hand. Ask him or her to decide which object feels heavier before giving the objects to the other partner to do the same. When both partners agree on which object feels heavier, have them record their answer. Have pairs exchange objects with another pair to repeat the activity.

© Houghton Mifflin Harcourt Publishing Company

Name _____

Learn the Math

About how many 🎲 does it take to balance a ✏️?

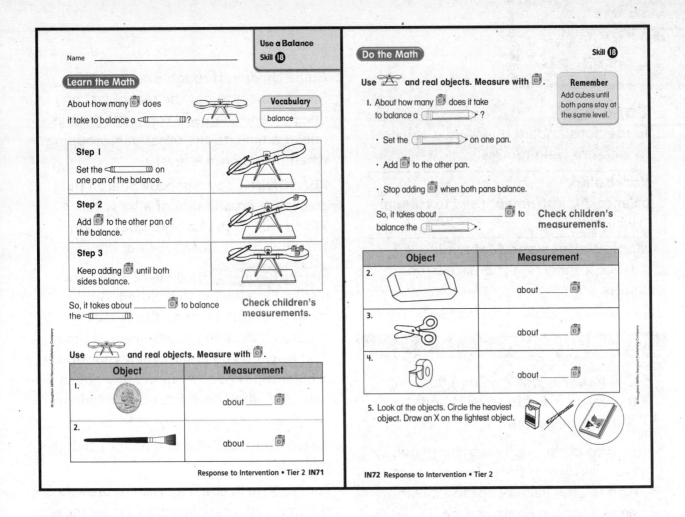

Step 1	
Set the ✏️ on one pan of the balance.	
Step 2	
Add 🎲 to the other pan of the balance.	
Step 3	
Keep adding 🎲 until both sides balance.	

So, it takes about _____ 🎲 to balance the ✏️.

Check children's measurements.

Use 🔺 and real objects. Measure with 🎲.

Object	Measurement
1. 🪙	about _____ 🎲
2. 🖌️	about _____ 🎲

Do the Math

Use 🔺 and real objects. Measure with 🎲.

1. About how many 🎲 does it take to balance a ✏️?

   • Set the ✏️ on one pan.

   • Add 🎲 to the other pan.

   • Stop adding 🎲 when both pans balance.

   So, it takes about _____ 🎲 to balance the ✏️.

   Check children's measurements.

Object	Measurement
2.	about _____ 🎲
3. ✂️	about _____ 🎲
4.	about _____ 🎲

5. Look at the objects. Circle the heaviest object. Draw an X on the lightest object.

Name _____

Learn the Math

About how many 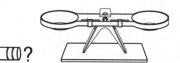 does it take to balance a crayon?

Vocabulary
balance

Step 1 Set the crayon on one pan of the balance.	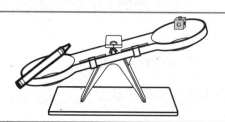
Step 2 Add to the other pan of the balance.	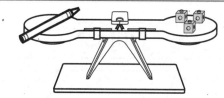
Step 3 Keep adding until both sides balance.	

So, it takes about _____ to balance the crayon.

Use and real objects. Measure with .

Object	Measurement
1.	about _____
2.	about _____

Use ⚖ and real objects. Measure with ⬛.

Remember
Add cubes until both pans stay at the same level.

1. About how many ⬛ does it take to balance a ✏ ?

   · Set the ✏ on one pan.

   · Add ⬛ to the other pan.

   · Stop adding ⬛ when both pans balance.

   So, it takes about _____ ⬛ to balance the ✏ .

Object	Measurement
2. ▱	about _____ ⬛
3. ✂	about _____ ⬛
4. 🎞	about _____ ⬛

5. Look at the objects. Circle the heaviest object. Draw an X on the lightest object.

Objective

To use nonstandard units to measure capacity

Vocabulary

capacity The amount that a container can hold

Materials

spoons, bowls, mugs, various containers of assorted capacities; dry rice or water

COMMON ERROR

- Children may have difficulty keeping track of how many units they have measured.

- To correct this, encourage children to keep a tally of the number of units as they measure.

Learn the Math page IN75 Read and discuss the problem with children. Guide them through Step 1. Make sure that children have the materials they need.

In Step 2, guide them to add one spoonful of fill material, such as rice or water, to the bowl. Ask: **Can the bowl hold more than one spoonful? Explain.** Yes; possible answer: the bowl is not full yet.

In Step 3, guide them to continue adding one spoonful of fill material at a time. Have them count the number of spoonfuls used to fill the container. Ask: **So, about how many spoonfuls will the bowl hold?** Answers may vary.

Guide children through Exercises 1–2. Check that children are counting the number of units they used to measure the capacity of each container.

REASONING Ask: **Why is the word *about* used when measuring?** Possible answer: the word *about* is used because a measurement is close to an amount, but is not an exact amount.

Do the Math page IN76 Read and discuss Exercise 1 with children. After they have measured a few spoonfuls, ask: **How do you know when to stop adding spoonfuls to the mug?** I stop adding spoonfuls when the mug is full, but not spilling over. Encourage children to measure the capacity of the mug and to count the number of units.

Assign Exercises 2–4 and monitor children's work.

For Problem 5, you may wish to provide children with a butter container and other containers. Encourage them to measure the containers and then find the one that holds more than the butter container.

Children who make more than 1 error in Exercises 1–5 may benefit from the **Alternative Teaching Strategy**.

Alternative Teaching Strategy

Materials: large container, paper cup, dried beans

Have partners measure the capacity of a large container, with a cup as a measuring unit. Have them use a large-sized fill material such as dried beans. Encourage one partner to measure while the other partner keeps track of the number of units they have measured. Invite partners to exchange containers with another pair and then switch roles to repeat the activity.

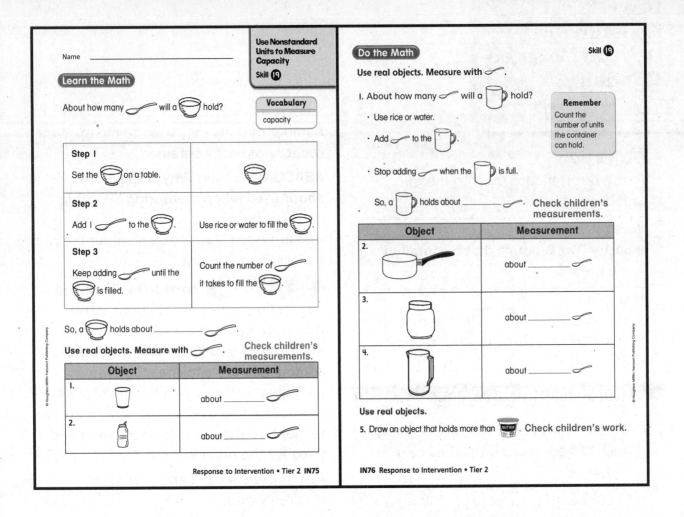

Name _____

Learn the Math

About how many 🥄 will a 🥣 hold?

Vocabulary

capacity

Step 1 Set the 🥣 on a table.	🥣
Step 2 Add 1 🥄 to the 🥣.	Use rice or water to fill the 🥣.
Step 3 Keep adding 🥄 until the 🥣 is filled.	Count the number of 🥄 it takes to fill the 🥣.

So, a 🥣 holds about _____ 🥄.

Use real objects. Measure with 🥄.   Check children's measurements.

Object	Measurement
1. 🥤	about _____ 🥄
2. 🍶	about _____ 🥄

Response to Intervention • Tier 2 **IN75**

Do the Math

Use real objects. Measure with 🥄.

1. About how many 🥄 will a 🍺 hold?

Remember
Count the number of units the container can hold.

- Use rice or water.
- Add 🥄 to the 🍺.
- Stop adding 🥄 when the 🍺 is full.

So, a 🍺 holds about _____ 🥄.   Check children's measurements.

Object	Measurement
2. 🍳	about _____ 🥄
3. 🫙	about _____ 🥄
4. 🫗	about _____ 🥄

Use real objects.

5. Draw an object that holds more than 🧈. Check children's work.

IN76 Response to Intervention • Tier 2

Name _____

Learn the Math

About how many spoon will a bowl hold?

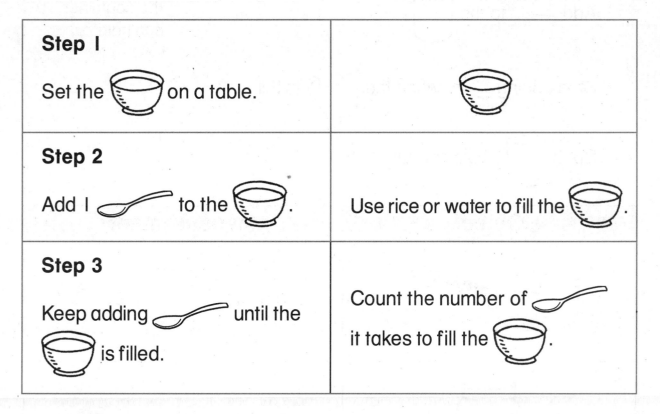

Step 1

Set the bowl on a table.

Step 2

Add 1 spoon to the bowl.

Use rice or water to fill the bowl.

Step 3

Keep adding spoon until the bowl is filled.

Count the number of spoon it takes to fill the bowl.

So, a bowl holds about _____ 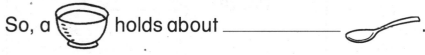.

Use real objects. Measure with .

Object	Measurement
1. (cup)	about _____ spoon
2. (bottle)	about _____ spoon

Use real objects. Measure with ◠.

1. About how many ◠ will a ☕ hold?

- Use rice or water.

- Add ◠ to the ☕.

- Stop adding ◠ when the ☕ is full.

So, a ☕ holds about _____ ◠.

> **Remember**
> Count the number of units the container can hold.

Object	Measurement
2.	about _____ ◠
3.	about _____ ◠
4.	about _____ ◠

Use real objects.

5. Draw an object that holds more than .

Nickels
Skill 20

Objective
To count by fives to find the total value of a group of nickels

Vocabulary
nickel A coin with a value of five cents

COMMON ERROR

- Children may not say the correct numbers when skip counting by fives.

- To correct this, have them practice counting by fives from 0 through 100 while looking at a hundred chart.

Learn the Math page IN79 Remind children that a nickel has a value of 5 cents or 5 pennies. Explain to children that because nickels have a value of five cents, they can skip count by fives to find the total value of a group of nickels. Invite children to look at the group of coins at the top of the page. Ask: **How many nickels are there?** 5 Ask children to name and trace the value of the first nickel. Ask: **What number do you say next when you count by fives?** 10 Guide children in counting and writing the count and the total value of the group of nickels.

Guide children in completing the second example. Encourage children to count by fives to find the total value of the six nickels.

Read the directions for Exercise 1. Guide children to count by fives as they count the coins. Have them write the total value on the line at the right.

REASONING Dimes have a value of ten cents. Ask: **How might you count to find the value of three dimes?** I can count by tens: 10, 20, 30.

Do the Math page IN80 Read the directions with children. Ask: **Why should you count by fives?** One nickel has a value of five cents. Have children practice skip counting from 5 through 50. Then guide children in completing Exercise 1. Be sure that children write each number that they count.

Assign Exercises 2–3 and monitor children's work.

For Problem 4, suggest that children draw eight circles to represent the nickels. Encourage children to point to each nickel as they count by fives to find the total value of Roger's coins.

Children who make more than 1 error in Exercises 1–4 may benefit from the **Alternative Teaching Strategy**.

Alternative Teaching Strategy
Materials: play nickels

Children will use nickels and count the value of a group of coins. Distribute a handful of nickels to pairs of children. Have one partner choose a set of nickels to display. The other partner should touch each coin and say the value of the group until the total value is found. Then have partners switch roles.

Learn the Math

A nickel has a value of 5 cents.

You can count by fives to find the total value.

Example 1

<u>5</u> ¢ <u>10</u> ¢ <u>15</u> ¢ <u>20</u> ¢ <u>25</u> ¢

So, the total value is <u>25</u> cents.

Example 2

<u>5</u> ¢ <u>10</u> ¢ <u>15</u> ¢ <u>20</u> ¢ <u>25</u> ¢ <u>30</u> ¢

So, the total value is <u>30</u> cents.

Count by fives. Write the total value.

1.

<u>5</u> <u>10</u> <u>15</u> <u>20</u> <u>20</u> ¢

Do the Math

Skill 20

Count by fives. Write the total value.

> **Remember**
> • The number you say last is the total value.

1.

• Count by _____**fives**_____

• How many nickels should you skip count? ___**3**___

<u>5</u> ¢ <u>10</u> ¢ <u>15</u> ¢

So, the total value of 3 nickels is <u>15</u> ¢.

2.

<u>5</u> <u>10</u> <u>15</u> <u>20</u> <u>25</u> <u>25</u> ¢

3.

<u>5</u> <u>10</u> <u>15</u> <u>20</u> <u>20</u> ¢

4. Roger has 8 nickels. What is the total value of Roger's nickels?

<u>40</u> ¢

Name _____

Learn the Math

A nickel has a value of 5 cents.

You can count by fives to find the total value.

Example 1

__5__ ¢   __10__ ¢   _____ ¢   _____ ¢   _____ ¢

So, the total value is __25__ cents.

Example 2

_____ ¢   _____ ¢   _____ ¢   _____ ¢   _____ ¢   _____ ¢

So, the total value is _____ cents.

Count by fives. Write the total value.

1.

_____   _____   _____   _____   _____ ¢

Count by fives. Write the total value.

1.

• Count by _____.

• How many nickels should you skip count? _____

_____ ¢   _____ ¢   _____ ¢

So, the total value of 3 nickels is _____ ¢.

2.

_____   _____   _____   _____   _____ ¢

3.

_____   _____   _____   _____   _____ ¢

4. Roger has 8 nickels. What is the total value of Roger's nickels?

_____ ¢

Objective

To tell time to the hour on an analog clock

Vocabulary

hour hand The shorter hand on the clock that shows the hour

minute hand The longer hand on the clock that shows the minutes

COMMON ERROR

- Children may confuse the hands of the clock.

- To correct this, demonstrate how the longer hand moves faster and connect the faster moving hand to the faster moving time—minutes pass quicker than hours.

Learn the Math page IN83 Read the introductory sentences with children. Guide them through identifying the hour hand and the minute hand on the clock. Ask: **How do you know which hand is the hour hand?** It is the shorter hand.

Write *10 o'clock* and *10:00* on the board. Explain that these are two different ways to write time to the hour. Point out that the number before the colon tells the hour and the numbers after the colon tell the minutes. Ask: **Why are there two zeros after the colon?** Possible answer: when the minute hand points to 12, it is 12 o'clock and no minutes.

Assign Exercises 1–2. Guide children in writing the time in the digital clocks.

REASONING Have children look at how they wrote each time. Ask: **What is the same about both times? Tell why.** Possible answer: both times are written with two zeros after the colon because both times are exactly to the hour.

Do the Math page IN84 Read and discuss Exercise 1 with children. Ask: **How do you know which hand is the minute hand?** It is the longer hand. Guide children in completing Exercise 1. Be sure that children write the hour before the colon, and two zeros after the colon to indicate the minutes.

Assign Exercises 2–5 and monitor children's work. Remind children to write the time in the digital clock.

For Problem 6, suggest that children circle the number word that tells the hour. Encourage children to draw a clock face to help think about where the hands will point for the given time.

Children who make more than 1 error in Exercises 1–6 may benefit from the **Alternative Teaching Strategy**.

Alternative Teaching Strategy

Materials: analog clockfaces (see *Teacher Resources*)

Have pairs use clockfaces to show and tell different times to the hour. Guide one partner to draw an hour hand pointing to a number and a minute hand pointing to 12. Have the other partner write the time below the clock. Then have pairs switch roles to practice several times.

© Houghton Mifflin Harcourt Publishing Company

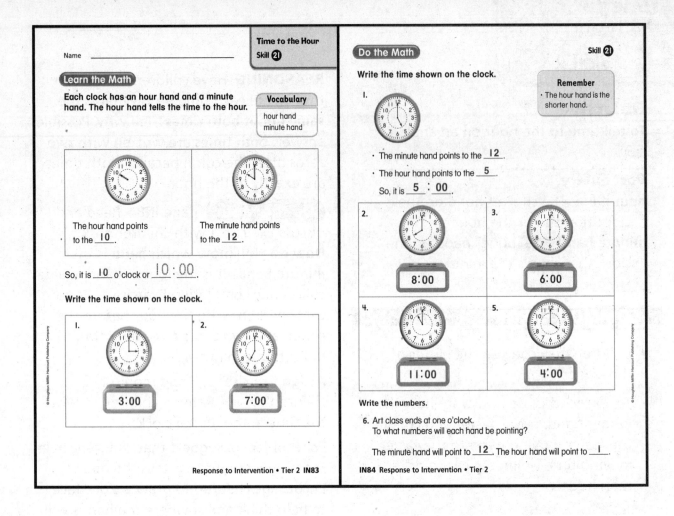

Name _____

Learn the Math

Each clock has an hour hand and a minute hand. The hour hand tells the time to the hour.

Vocabulary

hour hand
minute hand

The hour hand points to the **10**.

The minute hand points to the **12**.

So, it is **10** o'clock or **10 : 00**.

Write the time shown on the clock.

1.
3:00

2.
7:00

Do the Math

Write the time shown on the clock.

Remember
· The hour hand is the shorter hand.

1.
· The minute hand points to the **12**.
· The hour hand points to the **5**.
So, it is **5 : 00**.

2.
8:00

3.
6:00

4.
11:00

5.
4:00

Write the numbers.

6. Art class ends at one o'clock.
To what numbers will each hand be pointing?

The minute hand will point to **12**. The hour hand will point to **1**.

Name _____

Learn the Math

Each clock has an hour hand and a minute hand. The hour hand tells the time to the hour.

Vocabulary
hour hand
minute hand

The hour hand points

to the ____.

The minute hand points

to the ____.

So, it is ____ o'clock or __10__ : __00__.

Write the time shown on the clock.

I.

2.

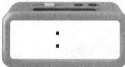

Write the time shown on the clock.

1.

- The minute hand points to the _____.

- The hour hand points to the _____.

   So, it is _____ : _____.

2.

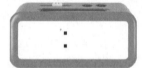

3.

4.

5.

Write the numbers.

6. Art class ends at one o'clock.
   To what numbers will each hand be pointing?

   The minute hand will point to _____. The hour hand will point to _____.

Identify Shapes
Skill 22

Objective
To identify two-dimensional shapes

Vocabulary
circle A plane curve equidistant from the center

triangle A two-dimensional shape with three sides and three angles

rectangle A two-dimensional shape with four sides and four square corners

square A rectangle with all four sides of equal length

COMMON ERROR

- Children may have difficulty remembering the names of two-dimensional shapes.

- To correct this, review the shapes and their names with children. Hold up a shape while they identify it. Write the names of shapes on the board. Have them draw and label shapes on a sheet of paper.

Learn the Math page IN87 Discuss the shapes with children. Guide them through each step looking at the shapes and asking them to describe each one. Guide them to see that while some shapes appear to be turned in a different direction, it does not change the name of the shape. If children have trouble identifying the shape, have them turn their papers so the shape appears upright. Point out to children that a square is a special kind of rectangle as it's four sides are all equal in length.

REASONING Say: **Suppose Dustin says that a classroom door is a square. Do you agree?** Possible answer: no; a classroom door is a rectangle because 2 sides have different lengths.

Do the Math page IN88 Discuss Exercise 1 with children. Guide them to identify the rectangles. Remind them that a square is also a rectangle. Ask: **Is a square also a rectangle? Why or why not?** Possible answer: yes; a square has 4 sides and 4 square angles, so it is a rectangle.

Assign Exercises 2–3 and monitor children's work.

Guide children to read the directions in Problem 4. Remind them that when it says, "Use at least 1 rectangle," it means that one of the shapes in their drawing should be a rectangle and that they can use more rectangles if they want to.

Children who make more than 1 error in Exercises 1–4 may benefit from the **Alternative Teaching Strategy**.

Alternative Teaching Strategy
Manipulatives: two-dimensional shapes

Partners will identify shapes to make simple pictures. Have the first partner use shapes to make a simple picture so that the other partner cannot see it. Then have the first partner give directions to the second partner to make the same simple picture using two-dimensional shapes. Children can use directions such as "Place a circle below the square." When finished, have partners compare their pictures.

Learn the Math

Color each square red.
How many squares are there?

Vocabulary
circle
triangle
square
rectangle

Step 1	
Look at the first shape. It is a circle.	
Step 2	
Look at the next four shapes. They are triangles.	
Step 3	
Look at the next two shapes. They are rectangles.	
Step 4	
Look at the last two shapes. They are squares. Color the squares red.	A square is a special kind of rectangle.

So, there are __2__ squares.

Do the Math

Use ✏. Color the shapes.

Remember
A square is a special kind of rectangle.

1. Color each rectangle green.

   G ○ ▷ G ○

   • Color the rectangles.

   So, there are __2__ rectangles.

2. Color each triangle blue.

   □ ◇ B ▭ B ○

3. Color each circle yellow.

   ◇ Y △ ▱ Y △

4. Draw a car. Use at least 1 rectangle, 2 circles, 1 triangle, and 1 square.

   Check children's drawings.

Name _____

Learn the Math

Color each square red.
How many squares are there?

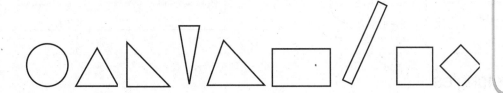

Step 1 Look at the first shape. It is a circle.	
Step 2 Look at the next four shapes. They are triangles.	
Step 3 Look at the next two shapes. They are rectangles.	
Step 4 Look at the last two shapes. They are squares. Color the squares red.	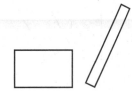 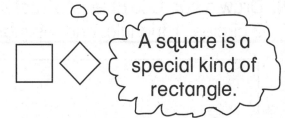 A square is a special kind of rectangle.

So, there are _____ squares.

Use 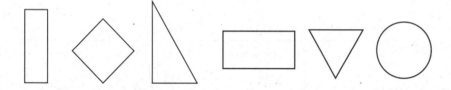 **. Color the shapes.**

1. Color each rectangle green.

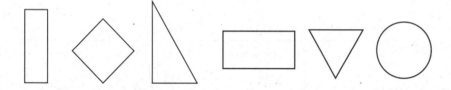

· Color the rectangles.

So, there are _____ rectangles.

2. Color each triangle blue.

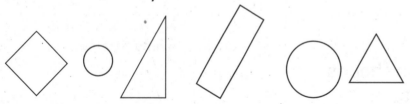

3. Color each circle yellow.

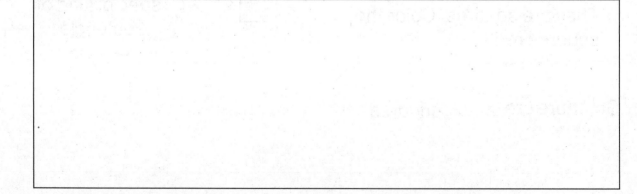

4. Draw a car. Use at least 1 rectangle, 2 circles, 1 triangle, and 1 square.

Objective
To identify what comes next in a growing pattern

Vocabulary
growing pattern A pattern in which a number or figure increases by a constant amount

Materials
number lines (see *Teacher Resources*)

COMMON ERROR

- Children may not be able to identify a growing pattern.

- To correct this, have them circle the numbers on a number line to help them identify how the pattern grows.

Learn the Math page IN91 Read the introductory sentences with children. Guide them through Step 1. Ask: **How does each part of the pattern grow?** It increases by one square. Guide children through Step 2. Point out that each answer choice has 5 squares. Ask: **How do you know which comes next?** Possible answer: the pattern grows by getting taller on the right side.

Read the directions for Exercise 1 and have children complete it. Ask: **How does this pattern grow?** Possible answer: each part increases by two dots. **What did you look for to decide what comes next?** the one with 7 dots

REASONING Have children look at Exercise 1. Ask: **If you continue the pattern to a fifth part, how many dots should it have?** 9

Do the Math page IN92 Guide children to point to each part of the pattern in Exercise 1 as they complete the sentences. Ask: **How does this pattern grow?** Possible answer: each part increases by 2 squares. **How do you know which part comes next?** Possible answer: I count by twos to know that the next part should have 8 squares. **Which is the incorrect choice?** the one with 7 squares **Why?** The pattern grows by two, not one.

Assign Exercises 2–3 and monitor children's work.

For Problem 4, suggest that children write the numbers in a row and identify the growing pattern to help them determine how many dots the next part of the pattern should have.

Children who make more than 1 error in Exercises 1–4 may benefit from the **Alternative Teaching Strategy**.

Alternative Teaching Strategy
Manipulatives: connecting cubes

Pairs will work together to use cubes to build growing patterns. Have partners agree on a number by which each part in the pattern should grow. Have one child show the first part of a growing pattern with connecting cubes. Then have the partner show the next part. Partners take turns showing parts of the pattern.

Name _____

Growing Patterns
Skill 23

Learn the Math

Each part of a pattern can grow. You can look at the number in each part to see what comes next.

Vocabulary

growing pattern

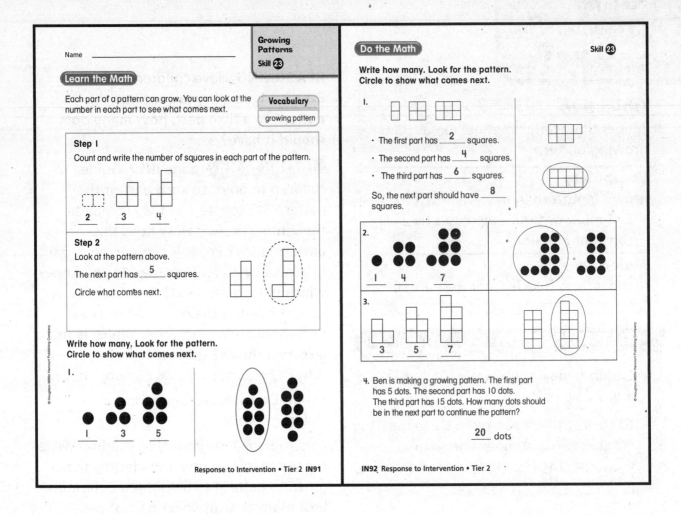

Step 1

Count and write the number of squares in each part of the pattern.

2   3   4

Step 2

Look at the pattern above.

The next part has __5__ squares.

Circle what comes next.

**Write how many. Look for the pattern.
Circle to show what comes next.**

I.

1   3   5

Do the Math

Skill 23

**Write how many. Look for the pattern.
Circle to show what comes next.**

I.

- The first part has __2__ squares.
- The second part has __4__ squares.
- The third part has __6__ squares.

So, the next part should have __8__ squares.

2.

1   4   7

3.

3   5   7

4. Ben is making a growing pattern. The first part has 5 dots. The second part has 10 dots. The third part has 15 dots. How many dots should be in the next part to continue the pattern?

__20__ dots

Name _____

Learn the Math

Each part of a pattern can grow. You can look at the number in each part to see what comes next.

Vocabulary

growing pattern

Step 1

Count and write the number of squares in each part of the pattern.

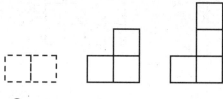

2 ___   ___   ___

Step 2

Look at the pattern above.

The next part has _____ squares.

Circle what comes next.

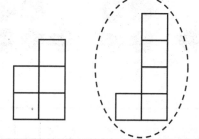

**Write how many. Look for the pattern.
Circle to show what comes next.**

1.

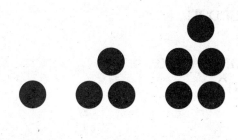

___   ___   ___

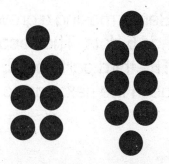

© Houghton Mifflin Harcourt Publishing Company

**Write how many. Look for the pattern.
Circle to show what comes next.**

1.

- The first part has _____ squares.

- The second part has _____ squares.

- The third part has _____ squares.

So, the next part should have _____ squares.

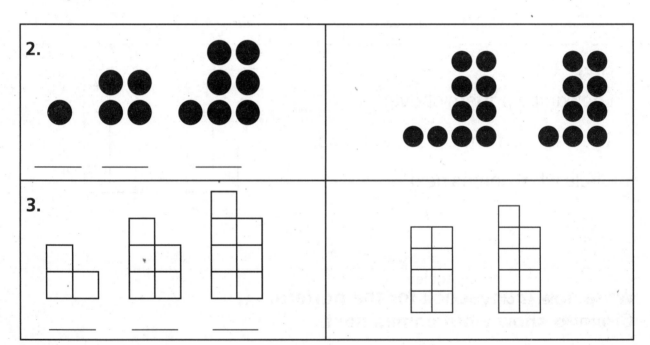

2.

_____ _____ _____

3.

_____ _____ _____

4. Ben is making a growing pattern. The first part
has 5 dots. The second part has 10 dots.
The third part has 15 dots. How many dots should
be in the next part to continue the pattern?

_____ dots

Act It Out •
Patterns

Problem Solving Strategy I

Objective
To use the strategy *act it out* to model skip counting patterns

Manipulatives
counters

COMMON ERROR

- Children may not understand how to act out a skip counting pattern.

- To correct this, help children understand that they need to show the same number of objects in each group to act out a skip counting pattern.

Problem Solving page IN94

- **What do I need to find?** Read through the story problem with children. Ask: **What is the problem that you need to solve?** to find how many flowers Mike will put in 4 cups

- **What information do I need to use?** Have children reread the problem. Ask: **What two pieces of information tell you the numbers to use in your pattern?** 2 flowers in each cup; 4 cups

- **Show how to solve the problem.** Guide children to act out the problem by showing 4 groups with 2 counters in each group. Then have children draw to show the groups of counters. Ask: **How many circles can you draw to stand for the cups?** 4 circles **How many marks can you make in each circle to stand for the flowers in each cup?** 2 marks in each

circle **How can you use a skip counting pattern to find how many flowers are in 4 cups?** I can skip count by twos: 2, 4, 6, 8. Ask: **So, how many flowers will Mike put in 4 cups?** 8 flowers

Assign Exercises 1–2 and monitor children's work. Remind them to find how many groups they need, as well as how many they need to show in each group. Encourage them to use a skip counting pattern to solve the problem.

Children who make more than 1 error in Exercises 1–2 may benefit from the **Alternative Teaching Strategy**.

Alternative Teaching Strategy
Manipulatives: connecting cubes

Have children use connecting cubes to act out skip counting patterns. Write a story problem on the board such as: **Joel puts 2 connecting cubes in each group. How many cubes will he put in 3 groups?** Have children connect cubes to form groups. Then have them skip count by twos to find the number of cubes in 3 groups: 2, 4, 6; 6 cubes. Repeat the activity with similar problems.

For answer page, see p. IN99.

Name _____

Problem Solving

Mike puts 2 flowers in each cup.
How many flowers will he put in
4 cups?

What do I need to find?	**What information do I need to use?**
Find how many flowers Mike will put in _____ cups.	_____ flowers in each cup _____ cups

Show how to solve the problem.
Use counters to act out the problem. Draw.

_____ flowers

**Act out the problem. Draw to show
what you did.**

1. Jen puts 4 roses in each box.
   How many roses in all does she
   put in 3 boxes?

_____ roses

2. Haley puts 3 leaves on each tray.
   How many leaves will she put on
   5 trays?

_____ leaves

Make a Model • Compare Numbers

Problem Solving Strategy 2

Objective
To use the strategy *make a model* to compare numbers

Manipulatives
base-ten blocks

COMMON ERROR

- Children may compare the digits with the lesser place values before the digits with the greater place values.

- To correct this, have children underline the hundreds digits in red, the tens digits in blue, and the ones digits in brown. Then have them use the colors to compare the digits, starting from red.

Problem Solving page IN96

- **What do I need to find?** Read through the story problem with children. Ask: **What is the problem that you need to solve?** to find whether the store has more toy cars or more toy trucks

- **What information do I need to use?** Have children reread the problem. Ask: **What two pieces of information tell you the numbers to use?** 243 toy cars; 175 toy trucks

- **Show how to solve the problem.** Have children use base-ten blocks to model the numbers in the problem. Ask: **How many hundreds, tens, and ones do you need to model the number of toy cars?** 2 hundreds, 4 tens, 3 ones **How many hundreds, tens, and ones do you need to model the number of toy trucks?** 1 hundred, 7 tens, 5 ones Have children

draw quick pictures of their models and label each model. Then have them compare the number of blocks in the models. Ask: **What happens when you compare the hundreds in each number?** 2 hundreds > 1 hundred Ask: **So, are there more toy cars or more toy trucks at the store?** more toy cars

Assign Exercises 1–2 and monitor children's work. Encourage them to use base-ten blocks to model the numbers and then draw quick pictures. Remind them that Problem 1 is asking for which is *fewer*, whereas Problem 2 is asking for which is *more*.

Children who make more than 1 error in Exercises 1–2 may benefit from the **Alternative Teaching Strategy**.

Alternative Teaching Strategy
Manipulatives and Materials: base-ten blocks, number lines (see *Teacher Resources*)

Have children use a number line strip and base-ten blocks to compare numbers. Prepare number line strips for children. Write two numbers on the board and have children locate these numbers on their number lines. Discuss how numbers on a number line show numbers in order from least to greatest as you move from left to right. Have children model the numbers with base-ten blocks. Help them to set the base-ten models above the number on the number line and then compare their values. Repeat the activity with different number line strips and another set of numbers to compare.

For answer page, see p. IN99.

Name _____

Problem Solving

At the store, there are 243 toy cars and 175 toy trucks. Are there more toy cars or more toy trucks at the store?

What do I need to find?	**What information do I need to use?**
Find if the store has more _____ or more _____ .	_____ toy cars _____ toy trucks

Show how to solve the problem.
Make a model. Then draw quick pictures.

more _____

Make a model to solve.
Then draw quick pictures.

I. There are 152 red kites and 127 blue kites on the shelf. Are there fewer red kites or fewer blue kites on the shelf?

fewer _____ kites

2. Jon's box has 196 marbles. Celia's box has 201 marbles. Whose box has more marbles?

_____ box

Act It Out • Length

Problem Solving Strategy 3

Objective
To use the strategy *act it out* to model length problems

Materials
inch ruler, yardstick

COMMON ERROR

- Children may have difficulty identifying the best measuring tool.

- To correct this, point out that shorter objects are more easily measured with a shorter tool and longer objects are more easily measured with a longer tool.

Problem Solving page IN98

• **What do I need to find?** Read through the story problem with children. Ask: **What is the problem that you need to solve?** to find which tool Juanita should use to measure the length of a pencil

• **What information do I need to use?** Have children reread the problem. Ask: **What are the two choices of measuring tools that are given?** an inch ruler, a yardstick

• **Show how to solve the problem.** Have children use measuring tools and a pencil to act out the problem. Have them decide which one of the tools is the better choice. Ask: **How can you decide which tool makes sense to use?** Possible answer: I can measure the pencil with both tools. Have children measure the

length of a pencil. Ask: **Which tool is the better choice? Explain.** Possible answer: an inch ruler is the better choice to measure the length of a pencil because the yardstick is too long. It is easier to use the inch ruler because the pencil is short. Have children draw or write their explanation. Ask: **So, which tool should Juanita use to measure a pencil?** an inch ruler

Assign Exercises 1–2 and monitor children's work. Encourage children to use measuring tools to act out the problem. Then have them draw or write to explain their choice.

Children who make more than 1 error in Exercises 1–2 may benefit from the **Alternative Teaching Strategy**.

Alternative Teaching Strategy
Materials: inch ruler, yardstick, classroom objects

Have partners work together to find classroom objects whose length can be measured with either an inch ruler or a yardstick. Then have them make a list of which objects are better measured with an inch ruler and which objects are better measured with a yardstick. Have partners tell why their choices make sense.

For answer page, see p. IN99.

Name _____

Problem Solving

Juanita wants to measure the length
of a pencil. Which tool should she
use: an inch ruler or a yardstick?

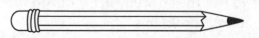

What do I need to find?	**What information do I need to use?**
Find which tool Juanita should use to measure a _____.	Juanita can choose: _____ or _____.

Show how to solve the problem.
Use the tools to act out the problem. Explain.

Juanita should use _____.

**Choose the better measurement tool.
Write or draw to explain your choice.**

1. Erik wants to measure the length
of a marker. Which tool should he
use: an inch ruler or a yardstick?

Erik should use _____.

2. Laura wants to measure the length
of a hallway. Which tool should she
use: an inch ruler or a yardstick?

Laura should use _____.

Problem Solving

Mike puts 2 flowers in each cup.
How many flowers will he put in
4 cups?

What do I need to find?	What information do I need to use?
Find how many flowers Mike will put in __4__ cups.	__2__ flowers in each cup __4__ cups

Show how to solve the problem.
Use counters to act out the problem. Draw.

(x x) (x x) (x x) (x x)

__8__ flowers

Act out the problem. Draw to show what you did.

Check children's diagrams.

1. Jen puts 4 roses in each box. How many roses in all does she put in 3 boxes?

__12__ roses

2. Haley puts 3 leaves on each tray. How many leaves will she put on 5 trays?

__15__ leaves

Problem Solving

At the store, there are 243 toy cars and
175 toy trucks. Are there more toy cars
or more toy trucks at the store?

What do I need to find?	What information do I need to use?
Find if the store has more __toy cars__ or more __toy trucks__.	__243__ toy cars __175__ toy trucks

Show how to solve the problem.
Make a model. Then draw quick pictures.

toy cars   toy trucks
                          more __toy cars__

Make a model to solve. Then draw quick pictures.

Check children's drawings.

1. There are 152 red kites and 127 blue kites on the shelf. Are there fewer red kites or fewer blue kites on the shelf?

fewer __blue__ kites

2. Jon's box has 196 marbles. Celia's box has 201 marbles. Whose box has more marbles?

__Celia's__ box

Problem Solving

Juanita wants to measure the length
of a pencil. Which tool should she
use: an inch ruler or a yardstick?

What do I need to find?	What information do I need to use?
Find which tool Juanita should use to measure a __pencil__.	Juanita can choose: __an inch ruler__ or __a yardstick__

Show how to solve the problem.
Use the tools to act out the problem. Explain.

**Check children's answers for reasonableness.
Possible answer: it is easier to measure shorter
lengths with a shorter tool.**

Juanita should use __an inch ruler__

Choose the better measurement tool. Write or draw to explain your choice.

Check children's answers for reasonableness.

1. Erik wants to measure the length of a marker. Which tool should he use: an inch ruler or a yardstick?

Erik should use __an inch ruler__

2. Laura wants to measure the length of a hallway. Which tool should she use: an inch ruler or a yardstick?

Laura should use __a yardstick__

Objective

To count forward using a hundred chart

Materials

crayons, hundred chart (see *Teacher Resources*)

COMMON ERROR

- Children may make counting errors as they move from one row to the next on the hundred chart.

- To correct this, explain to children how to read the numbers from left to right and from top to bottom.

Learn the Math page IN103 Distribute a hundred chart to each child and allow children to become familiar with it. Ask such questions as: **How is the hundred chart organized? What is the same in each row? What is the same in each column? How is each row or column different?** Guide children through the first example. Remind them to touch each number as it is counted. For the second example, explain to children that this problem does not start on number 1, but instead starts on number 46. Ask: **What is the last number you counted?** 59 Check that children color the box for the number 59.

REASONING Say: **Suppose Ben starts at 26 and counts to 39 on the hundred chart.** Ask: **If Ben colors the box for 40, is he correct? Explain.** Possible answer: he is not correct, because he should have colored the box for 39.

Do the Math page IN104 Read and discuss Exercise 1 with children. Explain that to count to 18 also means to stop on 18. Remind children to color the last number counted.

Assign Exercises 2–9 and monitor children's work.

For Problem 10, encourage children to use the hundred chart to help them circle the numbers Pam counts.

Children who make more than 2 errors in Exercises 1–10 may benefit from the **Alternative Teaching Strategy.**

Alternative Teaching Strategy

Materials: hundred chart (see *Teacher Resources*)

Prepare cutouts of number sequences taken from a hundred chart for partners to count. Have the first partner use the cutout number sequence to count the sequence. Then have the second partner place the cutout in the correct position on a complete hundred chart and count the sequence. Invite partners to select a new sequence and switch roles.

Learn the Math

You can use a hundred chart to count.

Example 1
Start at 1 and count to 23.

- Start at 1.
  Touch and count.
- Stop at 23.
- Color the last number
  you counted.

1	2	3	4	5	6	7	8	9	10
11	12	13	14	15	16	17	18	19	20
21	22	23	24	25	26	27	28	29	30
31	32	33	34	35	36	37	38	39	40
41	42	43	44	45	46	47	48	49	50
51	52	53	54	55	56	57	58	59	60
61	62	63	64	65	66	67	68	69	70
71	72	73	74	75	76	77	78	79	80
81	82	83	84	85	86	87	88	89	90
91	92	93	94	95	96	97	98	99	100

Example 2
Start at 46 and count to 59.

- Start at 46.
  Touch and count.
- Stop at 59.
- Color the last number
  you counted.

1	2	3	4	5	6	7	8	9	10
11	12	13	14	15	16	17	18	19	20
21	22	23	24	25	26	27	28	29	30
31	32	33	34	35	36	37	38	39	40
41	42	43	44	45	46	47	48	49	50
51	52	53	54	55	56	57	58	59	60
61	62	63	64	65	66	67	68	69	70
71	72	73	74	75	76	77	78	79	80
81	82	83	84	85	86	87	88	89	90
91	92	93	94	95	96	97	98	99	100

Do the Math

**Touch and count. Color the
last number counted.**

Remember
Touch each number
as you count.

1. Start at 3 and count to 18.
   - Start at 3.
   - Touch and count.
   - Stop at 18.
   - Color the last number
     you counted.
2. Start at 20 and count to 33.
3. Start at 36 and count to 49.
4. Start at 51 and count to 62.
5. Start at 68 and count to 85.
6. Start at 87 and count to 98.

1	2	3	4	5	6	7	8	9	10
11	12	13	14	15	16	17	18	19	20
21	22	23	24	25	26	27	28	29	30
31	32	33	34	35	36	37	38	39	40
41	42	43	44	45	46	47	48	49	50
51	52	53	54	55	56	57	58	59	60
61	62	63	64	65	66	67	68	69	70
71	72	73	74	75	76	77	78	79	80
81	82	83	84	85	86	87	88	89	90
91	92	93	94	95	96	97	98	99	100

**Use the hundred chart. Write the
missing numbers.**

7. 64, 65, _66_ , _67_ , 68, _69_ , 70, _71_

8. 72, 73, _74_ , 75, _76_ , _77_ , 78, _79_

9. 58, 59, _60_ , _61_ , 62, 63, _64_ , _65_

Use the hundred chart.

10. Pam counts to 79. She starts at 66.
    Circle the numbers she counts.

    80   (76)   65   (73)   63   86   (69)

Learn the Math

You can use a hundred chart to count.

Example 1
Start at 1 and count to 23.

- Start at 1.
  Touch and count.

- Stop at 23.

- Color the last number you counted.

1	2	3	4	5	6	7	8	9	10
11	12	13	14	15	16	17	18	19	20
21	22	23	24	25	26	27	28	29	30
31	32	33	34	35	36	37	38	39	40
41	42	43	44	45	46	47	48	49	50
51	52	53	54	55	56	57	58	59	60
61	62	63	64	65	66	67	68	69	70
71	72	73	74	75	76	77	78	79	80
81	82	83	84	85	86	87	88	89	90
91	92	93	94	95	96	97	98	99	100

Example 2
Start at 46 and count to 59.

- Start at 46.
  Touch and count.

- Stop at 59.

- Color the last number you counted.

1	2	3	4	5	6	7	8	9	10
11	12	13	14	15	16	17	18	19	20
21	22	23	24	25	26	27	28	29	30
31	32	33	34	35	36	37	38	39	40
41	42	43	44	45	46	47	48	49	50
51	52	53	54	55	56	57	58	59	60
61	62	63	64	65	66	67	68	69	70
71	72	73	74	75	76	77	78	79	80
81	82	83	84	85	86	87	88	89	90
91	92	93	94	95	96	97	98	99	100

Touch and count. Color the last number counted.

> **Remember**
>
> Touch each number as you count.

1. Start at 3 and count to 18.

   - Start at 3.

   - Touch and count.

   - Stop at 18.

   - Color the last number you counted.

1	2	3	4	5	6	7	8	9	10
11	12	13	14	15	16	17	18	19	20
21	22	23	24	25	26	27	28	29	30
31	32	33	34	35	36	37	38	39	40
41	42	43	44	45	46	47	48	49	50
51	52	53	54	55	56	57	58	59	60
61	62	63	64	65	66	67	68	69	70
71	72	73	74	75	76	77	78	79	80
81	82	83	84	85	86	87	88	89	90
91	92	93	94	95	96	97	98	99	100

2. Start at 20 and count to 33.

3. Start at 36 and count to 49.

4. Start at 51 and count to 62.

5. Start at 68 and count to 85.

6. Start at 87 and count to 98.

Use the hundred chart. Write the missing numbers.

7. 64, 65, _____ , _____ , 68, _____ , 70, _____

8. 72, 73, _____ , 75, _____ , _____ , 78, _____

9. 58, 59, _____ , _____ , 62, 63, _____ , _____

Use the hundred chart.

10. Pam counts to 79. She starts at 66. Circle the numbers she counts.

    80   76   65   73   63   86   69

Skip Count by Fives and Tens

Skill 25

Objective
To skip count by fives and tens using pictures

COMMON ERROR

- Children may miss a number as they are skip counting.

- To correct this, have children use a hundred chart to check their work. Children can count by fives or tens and circle each number. They can then count the circled numbers aloud.

Learn the Math page IN107 Read and discuss the first problem with children. Ask: **How are the groups of seeds you are counting alike?** Each group has the same number of seeds, 5. Have children count the seeds in each apple to check that each one has five seeds. Ask: **What number will you say first when skip counting by fives?** 5 Skip count aloud as a class to complete the problem. Ask: **What pattern do you see?** Possible answer: the digits in the ones place are 5, 0, 5, 0.

In the second problem, the pattern is different. Ask: **What pattern do you see when counting by tens?** The digit in the ones place is always 0. **How many toes are there in all?** 80

REASONING Say: **Jeff was counting by tens. He counted 5, 10, 20, 25, and 30.** Ask: **Did he count correctly?** no

Do the Math page IN108 Read and discuss Exercise 1 with children. Guide children to solve the problem. Ask: **Do all of the groups have the same number of oranges?** yes Discuss with children why this means they can skip count to find the total number of oranges. Ask: **What number do you skip count the oranges by?** fives

Assign Exercises 2–3 and monitor children's work.

For Problems 4 and 5, encourage children to draw a picture or use counters to help them count.

Children who make more than 1 error in Exercises 1–5 may benefit from the **Alternative Teaching Strategy**.

Alternative Teaching Strategy
Materials: 100 connecting cubes

Help children connect the cubes in trains of ten. Count by tens to find out how many there are in all.

Break each of the trains into two trains of five cubes each. Count by fives to 100. Have children explain how they can keep track of the trains they have already counted. Ask: **Why do you get the same number when you count by fives as you do when you count by tens?** Possible answer: they are the same cubes. I just counted in a different way.

Learn the Math

You can use a picture to skip count by fives and tens.

Skip count. Count the seeds by fives.
Write how many.

5, 10, _15_, 20, _25_, _30_ seeds

So, there are _30_ seeds in all.

Skip count. Count the toes by tens.
Write how many.

10, 20, _30_, _40_,

_50_, _60_, _70_, _80_ toes

So, there are _80_ toes in all.

Do the Math

Skill 25

Skip count. Write how many.

1.

_5_, _10_, _15_, _20_, _25_, _30_ oranges

- How many oranges are in each group? _5_

- When you count by fives, what is the first number? _5_

So, there are _30_ oranges.

2.

_5_, _10_, _15_, _20_, _25_, _30_, _35_ strawberries

3.

_10_, _20_, _30_, _40_ fingers

Remember
- Read the problem carefully before skip counting.
- When you count by fives, the digit in the ones place will be a 0 or a 5.
- When you count by tens, the digit in the ones place will always be a 0.

4. Liam has 5 groups of 10 pennies. How many pennies does he have in all? Count the pennies by tens.

10, 20, 30, 40, 50;

50 pennies

5. April has 7 groups of 5 gumdrops. How many gumdrops does she have in all? Count the gumdrops by fives.

5, 10, 15, 20, 25, 30, 35;

35 gumdrops

Name _____

Learn the Math

You can use a picture to skip count by fives and tens.

Skip count. Count the seeds by fives.
Write how many.

5,　　　10,　　　____,　　　20,　　　____,　　　____ seeds

So, there are ____ seeds in all.

Skip count. Count the toes by tens.
Write how many.

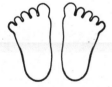 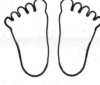

10,　　　20,　　　____,　　　____,

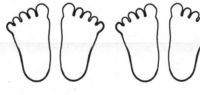

____,　　　____,　　　____,　　　____ toes

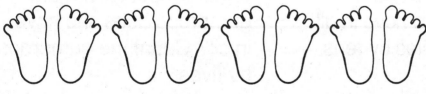

So, there are ____ toes in all.

Skip count. Write how many.

1.

____, ____, ____, ____, ____, ____ oranges

- How many oranges are in each group? ____

- When you count by fives, what is the first number? ____

So, there are ____ oranges.

2.

____, ____, ____, ____, ____, ____, ____ strawberries

3.

____, ____, ____, ____ fingers

4. Liam has 5 groups of 10 pennies. How many pennies does he have in all? Count the pennies by tens.

_____

_____

5. April has 7 groups of 5 gumdrops. How many gumdrops does she have in all? Count the gumdrops by fives.

_____

_____

Identify Three-Dimensional Shapes

Skill 26

Objective
To identify three-dimensional shapes

Vocabulary
sphere A round three-dimensional shape such as a ball

cube A three-dimensional shape with six square faces

cylinder A three-dimensional shape with two circular parallel bases and a curved surface

Manipulatives and Materials
three-dimensional shapes, crayons

COMMON ERROR

- Children may confuse a sphere and a cylinder.

- To correct this, remind children that a sphere is shaped like a basketball and a cylinder is shaped like a can of soup.

Learn the Math page IN111 Show children the three-dimensional shapes of a sphere, a cube, and a cylinder. Ask them to describe each shape in their own words. Guide children through each of the three examples. Encourage them to give some examples of other spheres, cubes, and cylinders found in the classroom or at home.

Guide children through Exercises 1–2. Check that they identify and color the correct shapes.

REASONING Say: Suppose Mia helped her father shop. She found an orange, a can of soup, and a box of cereal. Which object is shaped like a cylinder? the can of soup

Do the Math page IN112 Read and discuss Exercise 1 with children. Remind them to compare the objects to the cylinder and then color the objects that are shaped like the cylinder.

Assign Exercises 2–4 and monitor children's work.

For Problem 5, have children find an example of a sphere in the classroom before beginning to draw. Invite volunteers to describe and name the object they drew.

Children who make more than 1 error in Exercises 1–5 may benefit from the **Alternative Teaching Strategy**.

Alternative Teaching Strategy
Manipulatives and Materials: three-dimensional shapes for a sphere, a cube, and a cylinder; classroom objects shaped like a sphere, a cube, and a cylinder; paper bag

Place classroom objects in a paper bag. Invite a volunteer to choose one object from the bag. Ask that volunteer to describe and identify the kind of three-dimensional shape it may be without looking at it. Then have him or her reveal the object and describe how it compares to the three-dimensional shape.

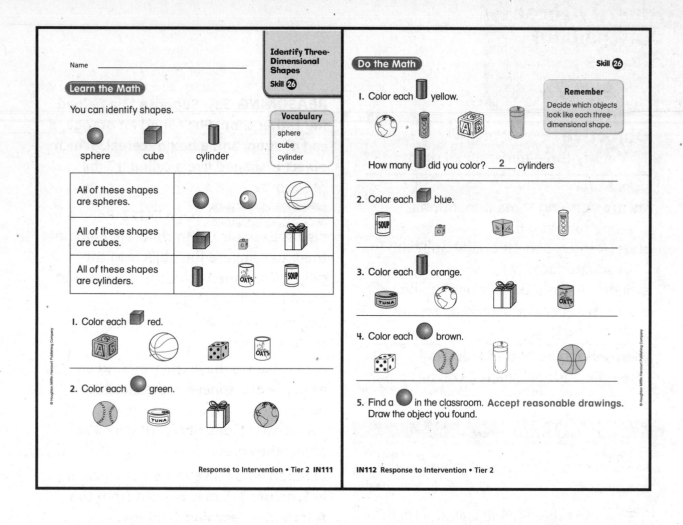

Name _____

Learn the Math

You can identify shapes.

sphere   cube   cylinder

Vocabulary
sphere
cube
cylinder

All of these shapes are spheres.			
All of these shapes are cubes.			
All of these shapes are cylinders.			

1. Color each ▢ red.

2. Color each ● green.

Do the Math

1. Color each ▮ yellow.

Remember
Decide which objects look like each three-dimensional shape.

How many ▮ did you color? __2__ cylinders

2. Color each ▢ blue.

3. Color each ▮ orange.

4. Color each ● brown.

5. Find a ● in the classroom. **Accept reasonable drawings.** Draw the object you found.

Name _____

Learn the Math

You can identify shapes.

 sphere

 cube

 cylinder

All of these shapes are spheres.	
All of these shapes are cubes.	
All of these shapes are cylinders.	

1. Color each red.

2. Color each green.

Do the Math

Skill 26

Remember

Decide which objects look like each three-dimensional shape.

1. Color each  yellow.

How many  did you color? ______ cylinders

2. Color each 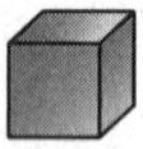 blue.

3. Color each  orange.

4. Color each  brown.

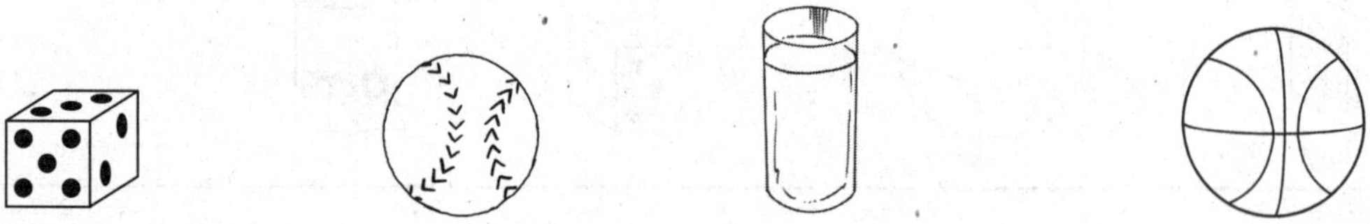

5. Find a  in the classroom.
Draw the object you found.